This book may be kept

FOURTEEN DAYS

A fine will be charged

WORKS OF BERTOLT BRECHT

The Grove Press Edition

General Editor: Eric Bentley

Previously Published

BERTOLT BRECHT
and
LION FEUCHTWANGER

THE VISIONS OF
SIMONE MACHARD

Translated and with a Preface by

CARL RICHARD MUELLER

An Evergreen Black Cat  *Book*

GROVE PRESS, INC. NEW YORK

Acknowledgments

I wish to express my gratitude to Mrs. Marta Feucht-wanger for her kindness and generosity in placing this play at my disposal for translation and publication. Without her sanction and approval this volume would not be possible. I am grateful also for the fact that she found time to make a most careful and intelligent comparison of my translation with the German original. At the same time she never, fortunately, demanded a slavish rendition of that original. Her cooperation and friendliness have made the task both fruitful and enjoyable.

My thanks, too, to Eric Bentley for his aid, advice, and constant concern with this translation from the very earliest draft.

Finally, my thanks and appreciation to the Fulbright Commission for affording me the time necessary to complete this translation in its early stages. The time spent on this Grant in Berlin, and, most importantly, with the Berliner Ensemble, an acquaintance with which is imperative for any Brecht scholar or translator, proved highly rewarding.

— C. R. M.

For Paul

— C.R.M.

Preface

As is true of many Brecht plays, *The Visions of Simone Machard* was not wholly his idea. It was during Brecht's American exile, in Santa Monica, California, that he was approached by the German novelist and his former collaborator, Lion Feuchtwanger, with what amounted to the germ for a play taking place during the Nazi invasion of France. Shortly before Feuchtwanger's suggestion to write the play, he had written a book titled *Unholdes Frankreich,* in which he described his experiences during his own exile in France, as well as the reaction of the French populace to its collapse, its hatred of the invader, the patriotic feeling of the entire people and the fierce disillusionment which ensued upon the French businessman's convenient collaboration with the enemy. Brecht was deeply moved by the book, and they worked together on the play between October 1942 and February 1943.

Yet Brecht's conception of the character of Simone differed considerably from that of Feuchtwanger's. This is best demonstrated by the novel *Simone,* which Feuchtwanger wrote a short time after work on the play ended.

It is instructive to note the differences between these two visions of the same material, both having sprung from the same source. Brecht, of course, being the playwright, had the major hand in the formulation of the play, while the novelistic treatment was solely Feuchtwanger's own. Nonetheless, Feuchtwanger's part in the play's composition must by no means be minimized.

Throughout the composition of the play, Feuchtwanger could never agree on one major point: the age of Simone. To Brecht's mind and feeling she had to be just this side of adolescence. In 1955 Brecht wrote to Feuchtwanger from East Germany that Simone must be "a child"; and on May 3, 1956, as Brecht lay in the hospital, just a few months before his death on August 3, 1956, he wrote to Feuchtwanger again: "The main thing in regard to a production of *Simone* is that the leading role must under no circumstances be played by a young actress (nor by an actress who looks like a child), but only by an eleven-year-old girl."

In Feuchtwanger's novel she is fifteen, and therefore an adolescent becoming sexually aware of herself and of her sexual role; furthermore, she has the power of conscience and deliberation. Each of these factors negates any semblance of naïveté. Feuchtwanger's Simone is a girl who knows her own mind and has thought considerably about the political and economic effects of a Nazi invasion. In her demands to the King in one of the novel's dream sequences she speaks of "class war," "sharp social contrast," and of "the export of capital." In a similar scene Brecht's Simone talks merely of the fact that France is in danger and demands that the King abolish taxes for her village (both of which she derived from her reading of the Joan of Arc book), and that the food pails of the soldiers be filled when they come asking for food (an incident she experienced just shortly before).

Feuchtwanger's Simone sells hoarded gasoline supplies at exorbitant prices, because she must, because she is working for her uncle who took her under his roof when she was left an orphan — she has an almost enforced obligation to carry through. Brecht's Simone works for

10

non-relatives in a hostelry-transport service, and sells not merely hoarded gasoline but overpriced food bags to the war fugitives, because she loves her employer with the love of a child for someone who is kind to her, and because in so doing she is keeping the job open for her hero-worshiped brother, André, upon his return from the war.

In the novel, Simone is not impelled to action by the vision of an angel whom she believes to be her brother; she is led on by rational thought and planning. In the play, Simone is child enough to see and believe the vision of her angel-brother who apprises her of the state in which France finds itself and commands her to "Go forth and destroy."

Simone, in the novel, goes to her action thus:*

> She trembled with impatience to carry out her decision, and at the same time she looked for excuses to postpone the deed. Again and again she groped in her pocket for the keys and the lighter. Again and again, without willing it, she pictured in her mind the course of the action and the consequences it would produce. It cost her great efforts to suppress her emotions . . . .

> She felt free and happy; she was filled with solemn serenity. It was her big day today; her life had a meaning. Her mission, her action stood before her, great and glowing . . . .

> She had reached the Porte Saint-Lazare. What did she really want here in the city? Why hadn't she rid-

---

* Lion Feuchtwanger, *Simone*, trans. G. A. Hermann; copyright 1944 by Lion Feuchtwanger. Reprinted by permission of The Viking Press, Inc. and Marta Feuchtwanger.

den directly to the loading-yard? Oh, yes, she needed an alibi. She would have to be seen in the city at the time of the action; she would have to be seen at the Deputy Prefecture. They all should believe secretly that the act had been done by the Planchard family, but nobody should really know it, so that no one would be entangled in it. That was very simple; she had calculated all that minutely. If it had not been necessary to establish an alibi, she would have been at the loading-yard long ago. She thrilled at the thought of it. She was racked and torn with impatience yet she feared the moment of the action and was glad of the excuse to postpone it . . . .

Presently, however, she drew up her shoulders uneasily. She seemed to feel the hard, small, wicked eyes of Madam upon her and she seemed to hear her soft, high, harsh voice: "I have spoken in vain. I have not succeeded in checking your impertinence and in putting you on the right way." No, she was not doing this out of impertinence. She was doing it because she was Simone Planchard, the daughter of Pierre Planchard.

The chapter ends with:

Her heart was filled with a great joy. Now the fire was running its prescribed course. Now uncle Prosper's name was safe from disgrace. Now Maurice had lost his bet. Now the gasoline and the trucks would not fall into the hands of the Boches.

For Brecht's purposes there are too many reasons here. His line of action for Simone is pure and uncomplicated (it is almost classic in its simplicity); there is no thought, no deliberation, no conscience, no fear — there is only love; with the result that this love towers triumphant over all the well-laid plans of the older Simone of the novel.

A primary virtue of the play over the novel is the strong visual element inherent in the material. Simone, in both the play and the novel, reads in her book about Joan of Arc, and has dreams in which she identifies herself with the historical Joan. Both contain anachronistic scenes of Joan-Simone in which past and present merge.

Let me quote two passages from the novel which correspond to one from the play in order to illustrate this point so central to both works. Simone is having one of her dreams:

> Then it is daylight and there is a battle and Simone is in the midst of it with her banner. The tanks approach lurching clumsily, all enemy tanks; there must be many thousands of them and they are all built of French steel. The sky is black with enemy aeroplanes and they are all built of French aluminum. But Simone waves her flag and no matter how many enemy tanks come, the poor people of France do not yield, and if hundreds are crushed down, two hundred more arise, and Simone continues to wave her flag . . . .

> And then the advance begins, and Simone is in the very first rank. But before her floats a great, bright figure; it flies ahead impetuously, its dress billowing with the speed of flight. And Simone sees that it is her goddess, her Winged Goddess of Victory. But this time she will not let her escape; now she has the opportunity to see her head and to find out who she is. Simone trembles with impatience. She forces her tank to its highest speed, but the clumsy vehicle rocks and lurches and cannot catch up with the flying figure. Sometimes Simone almost reaches her, but the goddess has only slowed her flight to accelerate it more than ever. It is plain — the winged creature is

13

teasing Simone. But now at last she turns her head in flight, she smiles at Simone, almost sportively, and — Simone knew it all the time — it is the pale, delicate head of Henriette.

A great bliss fills Simone, a happiness that almost breaks her heart. She feels light as a bird; she feels — victory; she feels — France; she feels — Liberty, Equality, Fraternity.

And then she is sitting in a movie, watching the newsreel. She watches a serpentine arrow on the screen that marks her advance from one town to another; she watches children exultant with joy because they have a school holiday on account of her victory; she watches all the world putting little flags on maps to mark the places she has taken, and they have to move the flags so quickly that they can't keep up with her. But Simone sits in the very last row of the movie and sees all that, and hides, hot with joy.

And then the alarm clock ticks more and more loudly and finally grows into a tremendous tolling of bells. That is because the Dauphin is being crowned in the cathedral at Rheims. The cathedral is badly riddled from shell-fire, and the sun shines through the roof, and everyone perspires in his Sunday clothes. But that makes no difference. The bells ring, the aeroplanes fly through the blue, crickets chirp, the band plays the "Marseillaise," and all join in singing.

Here is the corresponding passage from the play:

MAYOR (*resignedly*): Then how are we to conquer the English?

SIMONE: I must beat my drum now. (*She sits on the ground and beats upon an invisible drum. Each blow*

14

resounds as though it came from the earth itself.)
Come, you sailors of the Seine! Come, smithies of
Saint-Denis! You carpenters of Lyon, come! The
enemy is coming!

MAYOR: What do you see, Joan?

SIMONE: They're coming! Stay there, don't move!
Leading them on is a drummer with the voice of a
wolf, whose drum is spanned with the skin of a Jew.
And on his shoulder sits a vulture whose face is that
of a banker from Lyon. Close behind him on foot
comes Fieldmarshal Firebrand, a fat clown in seven
uniforms who looks like a human in none of them.
A newspaper canopy hovers over both these devils
so that I can recognize them. Behind them come
hangmen and marshals with swastikas branded on
their low foreheads. And behind them, as far as the
eye can see, are tanks and cannons and trains, cars
with altars built on them and torture chambers, because everything of theirs is on wheels and moves
quickly. In front of them all are the machines of war
and behind them the machines of plunder. Men are
mowed down with the wheat in the fields, but only
the wheat is gathered up again. Wherever they enter, cities are crushed beneath them, and they leave
behind them only a naked waste. But an end has
come to all that, for here stands Charles the King
and his Maid of God, Joan.

One final comment, on the endings of novel and play.
Both are reasonably similar as far as the action is concerned. Simone is sent to the Gray House, an institution
for the mentally defective, and a most infamous place,
where, as the Simone of the play cries out: ". . . their heads
get so big and the spit runs out of their mouth . . . . They
tie people up there!"

15

The novel ends with an undisputed sense of heroism, whereas in the play the sense is one of pathos. Simone's end in the novel is heroic because she goes without too much *final* resistance. To be sure, she, like the Simone of the play, cries out against her fate; but, writes Feucht-wanger: "She remembered her resolution. She would not permit her act to be robbed of its meaning. She would survive the Gray House. She would survive the evil. With this resolution her strength grew at a tremendous pace." She is led through the parting crowds from the room of her trial and out onto the square to the waiting vehicle. Then:

She turned around. With a long look, for the last time, she embraced the sunny square, the noble fa-çade of the Palais Noiret, the people whose faces were all turned towards her. So she stood; the door of the car had been opened for her, the gendarme had handed her belongings up, the interior of the car awaited her.

Suddenly the crowd, which had remained silent and motionless, stirred into action. Arms were raised waving to her, women and girls wept, the gendarme had come to attention, shouts sounded in her direc-tion: "Goodbye, Simone — goodbye, Simone Plan-chard — take care of yourself, Simone — so long, Simone — we won't forget you, Simone Planchard — we'll come and get you, Simone."

"Adieu," Simone said, with her fine, resonant voice; she had it under perfect control. "Adieu, my friends. Au revoir." She recognized how many were on her side. She thought: "I will have to stand the test; I must be the daughter of Pierre Planchard." She was

16

not afraid. Determination, born of realization, had given her strength.

Amid a storm of shouts she stepped into the old vehicle in which the uncouth woman was waiting for her. With a creaking, groaning sound the car started. Simone rode away into the black years of waiting, the salutes of solidarity in her ear, in her heart confidence that she would survive the Gray House.

Indeed this Simone has what it takes to survive the Gray House. She is fifteen, is no longer impressionable, and knows her own mind. Feuchtwanger's moving, though somewhat romanticized, apotheosis of her convinces one that she *will* survive.

With Brecht's Simone it is another matter. His Simone, though she does know her own mind, is nonetheless only eleven, is still highly impressionable, and still dangerously vulnerable. Brecht furnishes her no apotheosis (nor do I think he would have if he had revised the play in production or before his death), he makes no little heroine of her, and infuses her with no consummate composure in face of her fate. She is last seen being dragged off to the Gray House, crying in frantic despair.

And so Brecht leaves us to ponder this dilemma of his private vision, this bitter kernel of a vision naive, simple, uncluttered, but moving in a way that none of his other works are.

— CARL RICHARD MUELLER

*University of California,
Los Angeles*

17

THE VISIONS OF
SIMONE MACHARD

CHARACTERS

Mayor Philippe Chavez, *of Saint-Martin; Charles VII in the dream sequences*

Captain Honoré Fétain, *a wealthy wine merchant; Duke of Burgundy in the dream sequences*

Henri Soupeau, *owner of the Hostelry; Constable in the dream sequences*

Marie Soupeau, *his mother; Queen Mother Isabeau in the dream sequences*

Simone Machard, *a small half-grown girl; Joan of Arc in the dream sequences*

Maurice Prieux }
Robert Prieux } *two brothers employed as chauffeurs by the Hostelry*

Georges }
Père Gustave } *employees of the Hostelry*
Thérèse }

Madame Machard }
Monsieur Machard } *Simone's parents*

Colonel }
Sergeant } *of the French army*

German Captain

German Soldier

A Woman with a Baby

Two Refugees

A Man

Two Engineers

Angel

Townspeople, Refugees, Judges, Gray Ladies, etc.

Setting

The stage represents the Hostelry "Au Relais." In the back we see a low garage. To the right of the spectator is the Hostelry with its back entrance. To the left is the supply shed with rooms for the chauffeurs. Between the supply shed and the garage a rather large gate leads onto the street. The garage is quite spacious because of the Hostelry's transport business.

Time

The action of the play takes place in June 1940, in the small French town of Saint-Martin in the central part of France, on a main road between Paris and the south.

1
THE BOOK

(a)

GEORGES, *a soldier with his right arm bandaged, sits smoking a cigarette beside old* PERE GUSTAVE *who is busy mending a tire. The brothers,* MAURICE *and* ROBERT, *the two chauffeurs of the Hostelry, are staring up at the sky. One can hear the sound of airplanes. It is the evening of the fourteenth of June, 1940.*

ROBERT: They have to be ours.

MAURICE: They're not ours.

ROBERT (*calls across to* GEORGES): Hey, Georges, are they ours or German?

GEORGES (*carefully moving his bandaged arm*): Now there's no feeling in my upper arm either.

PERE GUSTAVE: Don't move it, that will only make it worse.

SIMONE MACHARD *enters, a half-grown child, with an apron which is too long for her and shoes which are too large. She drags along a very heavy basket of wash.*

ROBERT: Heavy?

23

Bertolt Brecht

SIMONE *nods and drags the basket to the base of the gasoline pump. The men watch her as they smoke.*

GEORGES (*to* PERE GUSTAVE): Do you think it's the bandage, Père Gustave? It's got stiffer again, since yesterday.

PERE GUSTAVE: Do as you're told.

SIMONE *leaves.*

ROBERT (*to* GEORGES): Can't you answer when somebody talks to you? It wears a uniform but doesn't bother looking up when planes come over. It's your kind of soldier who'll make us lose this war.

GEORGES: What do you think, Robert? My upper-arm feels numb now. Père Gustave thinks it's only the bandage.

ROBERT: I asked you what kind of planes those are.

GEORGES (*without looking up*): German. Ours never get off the ground.

SIMONE *has entered with a bottle of light wine from which she serves* GEORGES.

SIMONE: Do you think we're losing the war, Monsieur Georges?

GEORGES: Whether we lose the war or win it, I'll still need two arms. At least.

MONSIEUR HENRI SOUPEAU, *the owner of the Hostelry, enters from the street.* SIMONE *quickly hides*

24

the bottle of wine. SOUPEAU *remains standing in the doorway, looks to see who is in the courtyard, and motions in the direction of the street. A gentleman appears, covered with a large duster.* SOUPEAU *leads him through the courtyard, diligently concealing him from his personnel, and disappears into the Hostelry.*

PERE GUSTAVE: Did you get a good look at the gentleman in the duster? An officer. A colonel, in fact. Another one of our honorable deserters. They never want to be seen, but they can always eat enough for three.

SIMONE *has gone to her basket, seated herself on the base of the gas pump, and has begun to read a book which had lain on top of the basket.*

GEORGES (*over his wine glass*): Robert makes me mad. What the hell does he mean they're losing the war because of soldiers like me? I know a hell of a lot of others who haven't found me such a losing proposition, you can be sure of *that*. That man in Tours made a damn good profit off my shoes, and the man in Bordeaux off my helmet. My coat bought somebody a castle on the Riviera, and somebody else got seven race horses out of my leggings. So France had a field day off me a long time before the shooting ever started.

PERE GUSTAVE: And now we're losing it. Thanks to these deserters.

GEORGES: Sure, and how many planes are rotting away in hangars all over this country? Thousands of them, paid for and manned, tested and proven. But when we need them most they just sit there rotting away.

25

How many billions have we spent on fortifications, steel and cement, a thousand kilometers long, seven stories deep in the open field? But no sooner had the battle started than our good colonel stepped into his auto and retreated, his two carts of food and wine bringing up the rear. Two million men, ready to die, waited for orders; but the mistress of the Minister of War didn't agree with the mistress of the Premier, so there were no orders. Sure, our fortifications are rooted in the earth like trees, but theirs are on wheels and roll right on over us. Nothing can stop their tanks as long as they have the fuel they need. And they get their fuel from our stations. Tomorrow morning, Simone, they'll be waiting here in front of your pumps, pouring your fuel into their bellies. — Thanks for the wine.

ROBERT: You shouldn't talk about tanks when she's around. (*He indicates* SIMONE *with a nod of his head.*) Her brother's at the front.

GEORGES: She's got her nose stuck in a book.

PERE GUSTAVE (*to* ROBERT): How about a game of Belote?

ROBERT: I've got a headache. It took us all day to get the Captain's wine vats through those streams of refugees. It's like a mass migration.

PERE GUSTAVE: You mean the Captain's wine *isn't* the most important of the refugees?

GEORGES: The whole world knows he's a Fascist. Our good Captain must have got word from his cohorts on the general staff that things aren't going so well up at the front.

ROBERT: Maurice is furious. He said he's fed up with lugging those damned wine vats through the refugees. — I'm going to hit the hay. (*He leaves.*)

PERE GUSTAVE: These streams of refugees are enough to ruin any military campaign. A tank can make its way through every other swamp, but it always gets stuck in the human one. These civilians have set themselves up as the greatest evil this war has to face. They should have been got rid of at the start: get rid of the people or the war; we can't have both.

GEORGES *has seated himself beside* SIMONE. *He reaches into the basket of wash.*

GEORGES: You've taken the wash down dripping wet.

SIMONE (*continues reading*): The refugees are always stealing the tablecloths.

GEORGES: Probably for diapers, or rags to wrap their feet in.

SIMONE (*still reading*): But Madame always counts them.

GEORGES (*indicating the book*): Are you still reading about the Maid of Orléans?

SIMONE *nods.*

Who gave you the book?

SIMONE: Monsieur Soupeau. But I never get the chance

27

to read it. I'm on page seventy-two now, where the Maid has slain the English and crowned the King at Rheims. (*She reads on.*)

GEORGES: Why are you reading all this old-fashioned stuff?

SIMONE: Because I have to know what happens. — Monsieur George, is it true that France is the most beautiful country in the whole world?

GEORGES: Is that what the book says?

SIMONE *nods.*

Well, I don't know. I haven't seen the rest of the world. But they always say that the most beautiful land in the world is the one you live in.

SIMONE: Tell me, what is the Gironde like?

GEORGES: Well, I think they make wine there, too, the same as everywhere else in France. Some people even call France the great wine drinker.

SIMONE: Are there many skiffs on the Seine?

GEORGES: Maybe a thousand.

SIMONE: And in Saint-Denis, where you used to work — how was it there?

GEORGES: Nothing very special there.

SIMONE: But otherwise France is the most beautiful country.

GEORGES: Well, it has a lot of white bread, and wine, and fish. I have no complaints about the cafés with their orange-colored marquees. Or the markets with their fish and their fruits, especially early in the morning. I like the bistros where we drink our raspberry wine, and the yearly fairs and the ship launchings with their military music. They can all stay, every one of them. And who could say anything against the poplars where we go to bowl! — Do you have to go peddling your food at the assembly hall again today, Simone?

SIMONE: I only hope the engineers come before I have to go.

GEORGES: What engineers?

SIMONE: They're waiting for them in the kitchen, to feed them. They lost their field kitchen on the way, in the streams of refugees, and they're from the 132nd, too.

GEORGES: Your brother's with that outfit, isn't he?

SIMONE: Yes. They're going to the front. — It says here in my book, that the Angel desired the Maid to kill the enemies of France. That God wills it.

GEORGES: You're going to have nightmares again if you keep on reading that bloodthirsty stuff. Why do you think I took the newspapers away from you?

SIMONE: Monsieur Georges, do their tanks really push their way through piles of people?

GEORGES: Yes. And you've read enough.

He attempts to take the book from her. SOUPEAU
enters through the door of the Hostelry.

SOUPEAU: Georges, no one is to be allowed into the breakfast room. (*To* SIMONE:) You're reading on the job
again, Simone. I didn't give you the book for that.

SIMONE (*has eagerly begun to count the tablecloths*): I
only looked into it while I was counting the wash,
Monsieur Henri. I'm sorry, Monsieur.

PERE GUSTAVE: If I had been in your place, Monsieur
Henri, I would never have given her that book; it
does nothing but confuse her.

SOUPEAU: Nonsense. It's at times like these that she
should learn the history of France. These young
people now have no idea what it means to be a
Frenchman. (*Calling over his shoulder into the Hostelry:*) Jean, take the hors d'oeuvres into the breakfast room. (*To those in the courtyard:*) If you would
care to take a look in that book of hers, you might
learn what kind of Frenchmen we once raised here
in France. God only knows we could use another
Maid of Orléans now.

PERE GUSTAVE (*sanctimoniously*): And where will she
come from?

SOUPEAU: Where will she come from! From every corner
of this country. It could be anyone. *You! Georges!*
(*Indicating* SIMONE:) *She* could be the one. Any
child could tell us what's needed, that's how simple it
is. Even *she* could tell us.

PERE GUSTAVE (*examining* SIMONE *critically*): A little
small perhaps for a Maid of Orléans.

SOUPEAU: A little small, a little young, a little large, a little old; there's always an excuse with cowards. (*Over his shoulder into the Hostelry*:) Jean, have you served the Portuguese sardines yet?

PERE GUSTAVE (*to* SIMONE): Well, how would it be, Simone? How would you like a change of jobs? I'm afraid though there aren't many angels around anymore.

SOUPEAU: That's enough, Père Gustave. You will keep your cynical philosophy to yourself when you are around this child. Let her read her book without your filthy comments. (*Turning to go inside*:) Just don't let it happen again while you're working, Simone. (*He goes in.*)

PERE GUSTAVE (*grinning*): Isn't that something, Georges? Our scullery maid a Joan of Arc! But only in her spare time, of course. First they stuff our children full of patriotic ideas, and then *they* desert, walk out on their own men, like the Colonel in there. Or else they hide their hoarded gasoline in certain brickyards, instead of giving it to the army.

SIMONE: Monsieur Soupeau is doing nothing wrong.

PERE GUSTAVE: No, he's the father of good deeds. The only reason he gives you those twenty francs a week is so no one can say he leaves your parents penniless.

SIMONE: He lets me work here so my brother won't lose his job in the garage.

31

PERE GUSTAVE: With a gas pump attendant, a scullery maid, and a dish washer thrown in?

SIMONE: That's only because there's a war on.

PERE GUSTAVE: Yes, but it doesn't seem to be hurting *him* much, does it?

SOUPEAU (*appears in the doorway of the Hostelry*): Père Gustave, a half-bottle of Chablis '23 for the gentleman with the trout. (*He goes back into the Hostelry.*)

PERE GUSTAVE: So, the gentleman in the duster, alias the Colonel, requests a bottle of Chablis before France falls.

He goes into the storehouse shed. During the following scene he re-enters with a bottle of Chablis and goes into the Hostelry with it.

MADAME SOUPEAU'S VOICE (*from the second story of the Hostelry*): Simone, where are the tablecloths?
SIMONE *takes the basket and starts to enter the Hostelry just as a* SERGEANT *of the French army and* TWO ENGINEERS *enter the courtyard with a food pail.*

SERGEANT: We're supposed to get some food here. The Mayor's office said they phoned you about it.

SIMONE (*diligently, beaming*): I'm sure it's ready, Monsieur. Go right into the kitchen. (*To the* SERGEANT *while the* TWO ENGINEERS *go into the kitchen:*) My brother André Machard is with the 132nd, too, Monsieur. Do you know why we haven't received any letters from him?

32

SERGEANT: There's nothing but confusion up at the front now. We haven't heard from them either since the day before yesterday.

SIMONE: Have we lost the war, Monsieur?

SERGEANT: Of course not, Mademoiselle. Right now we have to guard against isolated tank attacks. We take it for granted the enemy will run out of gas soon and be left stranded in the streets.

SIMONE: I've heard that the Germans would never come as far as the Loire.

SERGEANT: I wouldn't worry about that. It's still a long way from the Seine to the Loire. The worst thing is all these refugees. We can hardly make it to the front. And we have to repair the bombed-out bridges before the reserves can get through.

The TWO ENGINEERS *enter with a half-empty pail; the* SERGEANT *looks into it.*

What the hell do you call this? Take a look at that, Mademoiselle — it's shameful! Not even half-full. This is the third restaurant they've sent us to. Two of them gave us nothing and here we get this.

SIMONE (*looks disconcertedly into the pail*): This must be a mistake. We have enough food here: lintels and even bacon. I'll tell Monsieur about this at once. You'll have all the food you want. Please wait. (*She hurries into the Hostelry.*)

GEORGES (*offering a cigarette*): Her brother's only seven-

33

teen. He was the only one of us here in Saint-Martin who volunteered. She's very close to him.

SERGEANT: The hell with this war, if you can call it that! Our army's treated like the enemy in its own country. And then the Premier says over the radio: "The army is the people."

PERE GUSTAVE (*has returned*): "The army is the people." And the people are the enemy.

SERGEANT (*hostiley*): What do you mean by that?

GEORGES (*looks into the half-empty pail*): Why do you put up with things like this? Get the Mayor.

SERGEANT: We know all about your mayors: they're all the same, they don't do a damned thing.

SIMONE (*returns slowly from the Hostelry; without looking at the* SERGEANT): The owner says the Hostelry can't give you anymore food; there are too many refugees.

PERE GUSTAVE: And we can't feed the refugees because the troops get it all.

SIMONE (*despairingly*): The owner is angry because the Mayor is always giving orders to feed soldiers and refugees.

SERGEANT (*tired*): The same excuse everywhere we go.

SOUPEAU (*steps into the doorway of the Hostelry and hands a folded check to* SIMONE): You may give the gentleman with the trout his check. Tell him that I charged him cost price for the strawberries and that your parents sold them to us. (*He pushes her inside.*) Well, what is it? Aren't you gentlemen satisfied? Maybe you'd like to put yourselves in the people's position for once and see what it's like. No matter how white they bleed us, we still get orders to feed you. There isn't a Frenchman alive who feels about France as I do: but — (*A large gesture of helplessness.*) It's only through sacrifice that I can keep this Hostelry open. Look at the help I have here. (*Indicating* PERE GUSTAVE *and* GEORGES.) An old man and a cripple. And then that half-grown girl there. I give them work only to keep them from going hungry. I can't feed the French army, too.

SERGEANT: And I can't let my men march all night on empty stomachs and face the enemy's fire for you! Fix your own damned bridges! I'll wait for my field kitchen if it takes till doomsday. (*The* SERGEANT *and the* TWO ENGINEERS *go off.*)

SOUPEAU: What can I do? You can't make everybody happy. (*Familiarly to his workers:*) Children, be glad you aren't plagued with having to run a hostelry like this. It's like fighting off wolves sometimes. And after all we went through to get the two stars after our listing in the guidebook! (*When* PERE GUSTAVE *and* GEORGES *show little interest in his troubles he grows angry:*) Stop your standing around like jackasses. (*Calls back into the Hostelry:*) Monsieur, the way is clear now.

The COLONEL *in the large duster comes out of the Hos-*

35

telry and goes toward SOUPEAU, *who accompanies him across the courtyard and into the street.*

COLONEL: Your prices are shameless, Monsieur! One hundred and sixty francs for a lunch!

GEORGES *in the meanwhile goes into the Hostelry and pulls out* SIMONE *by the hand, while her other hand covers her face.*

GEORGES: They left a long time ago. So you needn't hide in the hallway anymore. There's nothing you can do, Simone.

SIMONE (*drying her tears*): It's only because they're with André's company. The men at the front are waiting for help, Monsieur Georges, and the engineers have to repair the bridges before they can *get* help.

SOUPEAU (*re-enters from the street*): Foie gras, trout, leg of lamb, asparagus, Chablis, coffee and a cognac Martel '84! A meal like that at a time like this and they have the nerve to complain when they get their checks! And they have to be served in a hurry, too, because they can't wait to escape the battle zone. Officers they call themselves! Colonels! My God, what is France coming to! (*He looks at* SIMONE *with a guilty conscience.*) And as for you, the kitchen is none of your business! (*He goes into the Hostelry.*)

GEORGES(*to* PERE GUSTAVE, *indicating* SIMONE): She's ashamed because of the engineers.

SIMONE: What will they think of the Hostelry, Monsieur Georges?

GEORGES (*to* SIMONE): You're not the one to be ashamed, Simone. The Hostelry cheats and makes its own prices as sure as it rains and a dog farts. You're not the Hostelry, Simone. You don't laugh when they praise the wine, you don't cry when the roof falls in. You didn't pick out the linen. You didn't deny the food. Okay?

SIMONE (*unconvinced*): Yes, Monsieur Georges.

GEORGES: André knows well enough you're keeping his job here open for him. That's enough. And now go and visit little François at the assembly hall. But don't let his mother frighten you again with stories about stukas, or you'll start all over having nightmares about being in the war. (*He pushes her into the Hostelry; to* PERE GUSTAVE:) Too much imagination.

PERE GUSTAVE (*fixing the tire*): She doesn't like going to the assembly hall either. They scold her there because the food Soupeau makes her sell is too expensive.

GEORGES (*sighing*): If I know her, she'll stand up for Soupeau no matter what happens. She's a loyal one, Simone is.

SOUPEAU *enters from the Hostelry, calls toward the shed and claps his hands.*

SOUPEAU: Maurice, Robert!

ROBERT'S VOICE (*from the shed, sleepily*): Yeah?

37

SOUPEAU: Captain Fétain just telephoned. He wants the rest of his wine vats in Bordeaux at once.

ROBERT'S VOICE: Tonight? That's impossible, Monsieur Henri. We've been on the road for two whole days now.

SOUPEAU: I know that, I know. But what can you expect? The Captain says it's taking too long. Of course I know the roads are jammed and I don't like waking you: but — (*A gesture of helplessness.*)

ROBERT'S VOICE: The roads are blocked with refugees at night, too, and besides that we have to drive with our lights dimmed.

SOUPEAU: Well, it's the war's fault, not mine. Besides, we can't take chances with our best customers. Maman won't have it any other way. Now get ready. (*To* PERE GUSTAVE:) Will you hurry and finish that tire!

MONSIEUR CHAVEZ, *the* MAYOR, *has entered from the street, a briefcase under his arm. He appears quite disturbed.*

PERE GUSTAVE (*bringing* SOUPEAU'S *attention to the* MAYOR): The Mayor, Monsieur.

MAYOR: I'm sorry I have to bring this up again, Henri, about your trucks, that is. Yet I must insist now that you put them at the disposal of the refugees.

SOUPEAU: But I've already told you that I have a contract to deliver Captain Fétain's wine. I can't go back on my word now. Maman and the Captain were childhood friends.

MAYOR: "The Captain's wine!" Henri, you know how I dislike interfering in business matters. But I can no longer ignore your dealings with this Captain Fétain. We all know that he is a Fascist.

SIMONE *has returned from the Hostelry with a vendor's tray, loaded with large bags, tied about her; in her hands she carries two more baskets stuffed with bags.*

SOUPEAU: I suggest you be careful, Philippe, when you call the Captain a Fascist.

MAYOR (*bitterly*): "I suggest you be careful!" Is that all that you and your Captain Fétain can say to me, with the Germans already at the Loire? France is going to the dogs, Henri!

SOUPEAU: What? The Germans are where?

MAYOR (*sternly*): At the Loire. And our Ninth Army can't get through because Route 20 is blocked with refugees. I'm requisitioning your trucks, Henri, along with all the others in Saint-Martin. They will be at the assembly hall tomorrow morning to evacuate the refugees. That is an order. (*He takes a small red placard from his briefcase and begins to fasten it to the garage door.*)

SIMONE (*softly, frightened, to* GEORGES): The tanks are coming, Monsieur Georges!

GEORGES (*places his arm around her shoulders*): Yes, Simone.

SIMONE: They're at the Loire now, they're on their way to Tours.

GEORGES: Yes, Simone.

SIMONE: And they're coming here, too, aren't they?

SOUPEAU: Now I know why the Captain was in such a hurry. (*Shocked.*) The Germans at the Loire. That's horrible. (*He goes over to the* MAYOR *who is still occupied with putting up the red placard.*) You needn't bother with that, Philippe. Let's go inside. It's time we had a private talk with one another.

MAYOR (*angry*): No, we won't have anymore private talks, Henri. You can tell your employees that your trucks and your gasoline have been requisitioned by me. I've closed my eyes to this far too long as it is.

SOUPEAU: Have you lost your senses? How can you think of taking my trucks from me at a time like this! And there is *no gasoline* here, except for the little that's in that pump.

MAYOR: And the rest that you didn't declare?

SOUPEAU: What? Are you insinuating I am hoarding gasoline against the law? (*Furiously.*) Père Gustave, are we illegally hoarding gasoline?

PERE GUSTAVE *chooses not to hear and busies himself with rolling the tire into the garage.*

(*Shouting:*) Maurice! Robert! Come down here at once! Père Gustave!

PERE GUSTAVE *stops.*

Answer my question! *Are* we or *are we not* hoarding illegal gasoline?

40

PERE GUSTAVE: I know nothing about it. (*To* SIMONE *who is staring at him:*) Get to work and stop listening to other people's talk.

SOUPEAU: Maurice! Robert! Where are you?

MAYOR: If you have no extra gasoline, how do you propose to deliver the Captain's wine?

SOUPEAU: An excellent leading question, Monsieur. Allow me to answer: I am delivering the Captain's wine with the Captain's *own* gasoline. Georges, what do you know about any illegal gasoline we're hoarding here?

GEORGES (*looking at his arm*): I just got back from the front a couple days ago.

SOUPEAU: Quite right; then you can't be expected to know anything. But here are Maurice and Robert.
MAURICE *and* ROBERT *have entered.*

Maurice, Robert! Monsieur Chavez has accused the Hostelry of hiding gasoline. I am asking you in front of Monsieur Chavez: *Is this true?*

They hesitate.

MAYOR: Maurice, Robert: you know who I am. I am not a policeman and I dislike interfering in business matters. But France needs all the gasoline she can lay her hands on now, and I beg you to admit to our people that there *is gasoline* here. I know you both for honorable men.

SOUPEAU: Well?

MAURICE (*darkly*): We know nothing about any gasoline.

MAYOR: So, that's your answer. (*To* SIMONE:) And you have a brother at the front, haven't you? And even you won't admit that there's gasoline here.

SIMONE *stands motionlessly, then begins to cry.*

SOUPEAU: And now you want to make a half-grown child testify against me! You have no right, Monsieur, to try to undermine this child's respect for her employer. (*To* SIMONE:) Go on now, Simone.

MAYOR (*tired*): Are you still peddling your food at the assembly hall, Henri? And you couldn't give the engineers enough for their supper. No wonder the refugees never get on, what with people everywhere cheating them out of every sou they have.

SOUPEAU: I'm not running a charity here, Monsieur, I operate a hostelry and a restaurant.

MAYOR: Yes, I know. — Only a miracle can save France now. It's rotten to the core. (*He goes out.*)

A silence ensues.

SOUPEAU: Forward, Simone! Hip-hop!

SIMONE *goes slowly, unsurely, often looking behind her toward the door of the courtyard. On the way, the book which she has hidden in her food tray falls to the ground. She picks it up shyly and leaves the courtyard, carrying her bags and her baskets.*

THE FIRST DREAM
OF
SIMONE MACHARD

It is the night of the fourteenth of June. Music. The ANGEL
*emerges from the darkness. He stands on the roof of the
garage; his face is a gilt color, without expression. In
his hands he holds a small drum, and calls out three times
with a loud voice.*

ANGEL: Joan! Joan! Joan!

> *The stage grows light again.* SIMONE *is seen standing
> in the empty courtyard of the Hostelry looking up at
> the* ANGEL. *She carries a washbasket in her arms.*

ANGEL: Joan, Daughter of France, the foe must be put
    to rout
Or France will fall to the enemy in two weeks' time with-
    out doubt.
Therefore the Lord God has sought about for aid
And thus he came upon you, Joan, His little maid.
And herewith I give you a drum, sent to you from God
With which you must waken the people from their busi-
    ness and daily plod.

But know that it will sound only when laid on the earth
As though the ground of France alone could give the
    sound birth.
Sound your drum now, call rich and poor with your hand
So that the sons of France may take pity on their land.
Tell the sailors of the Seine that our sons need their skiffs
    to be loaned.
And that bread and wine they'll need from the farmers of
    Gironde.
The smithies of Saint-Denis shall build her iron tanks
The carpenters of Lyon destroy bridges before enemy
    ranks.
Tell them that France, their mother, who carried them
    in her womb
France whom they have mocked and struck in her hour of
    gloom
France, the great worker, France, the great drinker of
    wine
Needs them in her hour of peril. Go now and bring them
    in line.

SIMONE looks around to see if there are others behind her.

SIMONE: Must *I* do it, Monsieur? Don't you think I'm too
small for a Joan of Arc?

ANGEL: No.

SIMONE: Then I'll do it.

ANGEL: It will not be easy.

The ANGEL speaks a short sentence in a dream language which the spectator does not understand.

44

SIMONE (*timidly*): Are you my brother André?

The ANGEL *is silent.*

How are you?

The ANGEL *disappears.* GEORGES *comes sauntering in from the darkness of the garage and brings* SIMONE *his helmet and his side arms.*

GEORGES: My helmet and sword. You'll need them. It's hardly a job for you, but all Soupeau has is a cripple and a half-grown girl. Don't you worry about your work here. Listen; the tanks are driving through the town like sausage grinders. It's no wonder your brother's an angel already!

SIMONE (*taking his helmet and sword*): Shall I polish them for you, Monsieur Georges?

GEORGES: No, as the Maid of Orléans you'll need them.

SIMONE (*puts on the helmet*): That's true. And I must go to the King at Orléans at once, that's thirty kilometers — tanks can do seventy an hour — and I have holes in my shoes, I get new ones at Easter. (*Turns to go.*) Please wave to me, Monsieur Georges, otherwise I'll be afraid. War is such an old-fashioned bloody business.

GEORGES *attempts to wave his bandaged arm, then disappears.* SIMONE *sets out on her journey toward Orléans by marching around in a small circle.*

SIMONE *sings loudly:*

> As I went off to Saint-Nazaire
> I went without my trousers.
> Soon a great commotion rose:
> Where, pray, are your trousers?
> Said I to them: At Saint-Nazaire
> The heavens are too blue
> And the oats are all too high
> And the heavens are too blue.

The chauffeurs MAURICE *and* ROBERT *enter suddenly behind her. They are dressed in medieval armor, though they wear it on top of their overalls.*

SIMONE: What are you doing here? Why are you following me?

ROBERT: We're following you because we're your bodyguards. But I'd rather you didn't sing that song, it doesn't seem to fit. We're betrothed to you, Joan, so behave yourself properly.

SIMONE: Am I betrothed to Maurice, too?

MAURICE: Yes, secretly.

PERE GUSTAVE *enters and meets them. He is dressed in a primitive medieval suit of armor. He looks away and tries to pass them.*

SIMONE: Père Gustave!

PERE GUSTAVE: Leave me alone, you. Making me tend cannons at *my* age! The nerve! Live on your tips and die for France!

SIMONE (*softly*): But France, your mother, is in danger.

PERE GUSTAVE: My mother was Madame Poirot, a wash-woman. She was in danger of consumption. But what could I do? I didn't have money for a hundred different medicines.

SIMONE (*shouts*): Then I command you, in the name of God and of the Angel, that you return and take charge of the cannons! (*Placatingly.*) I'll polish them for you.

PERE GUSTAVE: Well, that's different. Here, carry my spear. (*He hands her his spear and trots along with them.*)

MAURICE: How much longer, Simone? But I suppose it's all for the good of the rich.

He speaks to her in the dream language, and SIMONE *replies in the same way. She speaks with great persuasiveness;* MAURICE, *having understood her, replies:*

You're absolutely right. Good, let's go.

ROBERT: You're limping, Simone. The arms are too heavy for you.

SIMONE (*suddenly very exhausted*): I'm sorry. It's only because I didn't have a proper breakfast. (*She remains standing and dries her perspiration.*) I'll be all right soon. Robert, do you remember what I was to tell the King?

ROBERT *says something to her in the dream language, something no one else understands; then:*

47

ROBERT: That's all.

SIMONE: Of course, thank you. Look there, you can already to see the towers of Orléans.

The COLONEL *of the first scene enters in a suit of armor, his duster thrown over it. He steals across the yard and out.*

PERE GUSTAVE: It's off to a good start, I see. The marshals are already deserting the city.

SIMONE: Why are the streets so empty, Père Gustave?

PERE GUSTAVE: They're probably all at supper.

SIMONE: And why aren't they sounding the alarm bells if the enemy's coming?

PERE GUSTAVE: They were probably sent to Bordeaux at the request of Captain Fétain.

SOUPEAU *appears in the doorway of the Hostelry. He wears a helmet with a red plume; something like steel glitters across his chest.*

SOUPEAU: Joan, you are to take the black-market bags to the assembly hall at once, do you hear me?

SIMONE: But, Monsieur Henri, France, our Mother, is in danger, the Germans are at the Loire, and I must speak with the King.

SOUPEAU: That's outrageous! The Hostelry is doing its

utmost. And you will do well to remember the respect due your employer.

A man in purple dress appears from the garage.

SIMONE (*proudly*): Oh, look Monsieur Henri, there's the King! Charles the Seventh!

The man in purple dress shows himself to be the MAYOR *with the royal robes thrown over his suit.*

MAYOR: Good day to you, Joan.

SIMONE (*astounded*): Are *you* the King?

MAYOR: Yes, I'm official. I'm requisitioning the delivery trucks. We must have a private talk with one another, Joan.

The chauffeurs MAURICE *and* ROBERT, PERE GUSTAVE *and* SOUPEAU *disappear into the dark.* SIMONE *and the* MAYOR *seat themselves on the base of the gas pump.*

MAYOR: It's all over, Joan. The Marshal has left on a trip without a word, without even leaving his address. I've written to the Constable for cannons, but the letter with the Royal Seal was returned unopened. The Master of the Horses claims he's been wounded in the arm, but as yet no one has seen the wound. It's all rotten to the core. (*He weeps.*) And I know why you've come: to reproach me for being a weakling. And that's what I am. But what about you, Joan? First of all I want you to tell me where the black-market gasoline is hidden!

SIMONE: In the brickyard, of course.

MAYOR: I know I've closed my eyes to it up to now, bu[t]
you're cheating those refugees out of every sou the[y]
have with your overpriced food bags.

SIMONE: I do it only to keep an Angel's job open for him[,]
Your Majesty.

MAYOR: And the chauffeurs are rescuing the Captain'[s]
wine instead of the refugees because of *their* jobs?

SIMONE: And because Monsieur Soupeau claimed them a[s]
essential workers, you know.

MAYOR: Yes, it's the Soupeaus and the aristocracy that
have to thank for my gray hairs. The aristocracy i[s]
against the King. That's the way it reads in you[r]
book, too. While behind you stand the people, espe[-]
cially Maurice. Can't we come to an agreement, Joan[,]
just you and I?

SIMONE: Why not, Your Majesty? (*Hesitantly.*) Onl[y]
you'll have to take a firmer hand in business matter[s]
and see that the food pails are always full.

MAYOR: I'll see what I can do. In any case I'll have t[o]
be careful, otherwise they're liable to cut my roya[l]
salary. I've always been the man to close his eye[s]
to everything, so that when I do have something t[o]
say nobody pays any attention to me. I'm suppose[d]
to do all the unpleasantries. Now the engineers, fo[r]
example. Instead of taking their food from you b[y]
force, they come to me: "Fix your own damne[d]
bridges. We'll wait for our field kitchen." Am I t[o]

be surprised when the Duke of Burgundy deserts me for the English?

SOUPEAU (*stands in the doorway*): I understand you are dissatisfied, Your Majesty. Perhaps you'd like to put yourself in the people's position for once and see what it's like. They're almost bled white. There isn't a Frenchman alive who feels about France as I do. But — (*A large gesture of helplessness and he goes off.*)

MAYOR (*resignedly*): Then how are we to conquer the English?

SIMONE: I must beat my drum. (*She sits on the ground and beats upon an invisible drum. Each blow resounds as though it came from the earth itself.*) Come, you sailors of the Seine! Come, smithies of Saint-Denis! You carpenters of Lyon, come! The enemy is coming!

MAYOR: What do you see, Joan?

SIMONE: They're coming! Stay there, don't move! Leading them on is a drummer with the voice of a wolf, whose drum is spanned with the skin of a Jew. And on his shoulder sits a vulture whose face is that of a banker from Lyon. Close behind him on foot comes Fieldmarshal Firebrand, a fat clown in seven uniforms who looks like a human in none of them. A newspaper canopy hovers over both these devils so that I can recognize them. Behind them come hangmen and marshals with swastikas branded on their low foreheads. And behind them, as far as the eye can see, are tanks and cannons and trains, cars with altars built on them and torture chambers, because everything of theirs is on wheels and moves swiftly. In front of them all are the machines of war and behind them the machines of plunder. Men are mowed down with the wheat in the fields, but only the wheat is gathered up again. Wherever they enter, cities are crushed beneath them, and they leave behind them only a naked waste. But an end has come to all that, for here stand Charles the King and his Maid of God, Joan.

All Frenchmen have found their way there, those who have already entered and those who are still to enter, all with medieval arms and dressed in portions of armor.

SIMONE (*radiantly*): There, you see, my King, they have all come.

MAYOR: Not all, Joan. For example, I don't see my mother Isabeau here. And the Constable went away angry, too.

SIMONE: Don't be afraid. I must crown you King of France, so that unity may once again rule this land. And look, I've even brought your crown with me. (*She takes a crown from the basket.*)

MAYOR: But who will play cards with me if the Constable stays away?

SIMONE *replies in the dream language. Then she places the crown on the head of the* MAYOR. *The* ENGINEERS *appear in the background and strike on their*

52

food kettles with their ladles. A great ringing of bells ensues.

MAYOR: What bells are those?

SIMONE: The bells of the Cathedral of Rheims.

MAYOR: But aren't those the engineers I sent to the Hostelry for food?

SIMONE: But they received nothing, Your Majesty. That's why their kettles are empty. Their kettles are your coronation chimes, my King.

The MAYOR replies in the dream language.

ALL: Long live the King and Joan the Maid who crowned him!

MAYOR (*to* SIMONE): Many thanks, Joan, you have saved France!

The stage grows dark. The voice of a radio announcer merges with the sounds of confused music.

2

THE HANDSHAKE

(a)

The time is early morning. The chauffeurs MAURICE *and* ROBERT, PERE GUSTAVE *and the soldier* GEORGES *are at breakfast. A radio is heard from the Hostelry.*

VOICE OF A RADIO ANNOUNCER: We repeat the intelligence of the Ministry of War reported at three-thirty this morning. As a consequence of the unexpected passage of German tank formations across the Loire, new streams of refugees are known to have flooded strategic military routes in central parts of France. The civilian population is urgently requested to remain where it is in order that routes may be kept free for the passage of relief troops.

MAURICE: It's time to get out of here.

GEORGES: The headwaiter and the others took off at five this morning, after spending all night loading the china into boxes. Soupeau threatened them with calling the police. But it didn't do much good.

ROBERT (*to* GEORGES): Why didn't you wake us right away, too?

GEORGES *is silent.*

MAURICE: Soupeau wouldn't let you, uh? (*He laughs.*)

ROBERT: Aren't you going to leave here, too, Georges?

GEORGES: No. I'm going to take my uniform off and stay. There's food here, and besides that I don't think my arm will ever be much good anymore.

SOUPEAU *enters busily from the Hostelry. He is scrupulously dressed.* SIMONE *enters behind him dragging a trunk.*

SOUPEAU (*clapping his hands*): Maurice, Robert, Gustave, let's go, let's go. You have to load the china up. Everything in the storeroom has to be put on the trucks. Pack the hams in salt. But load the wine on first. Drink your coffee later: this is war. We're going to Bordeaux.

They continue their breakfast. MAURICE *enters.*

SOUPEAU: What's the matter now? Didn't you hear me? We've got to get packed and loaded up.

MAURICE (*lazily*): The trucks have been requisitioned.

SOUPEAU: Requisitioned? Nonsense! (*With a large gesture.*) That was yesterday's order. The German tanks are on their way toward Saint-Martin. That changes everything. Yesterday's laws mean nothing today.

PERE GUSTAVE (*in a low voice*): I second that.

SOUPEAU: Take that cup from your mouth when I talk to you!

> SIMONE *has set down the bags, and during this last exchange has stolen back into the Hostelry.*

MAURICE: More coffee, Robert?

ROBERT: Sure. You never know where the next cup will come from.

SOUPEAU (*swallowing his anger*): Be reasonable. Won't you help your employer save his personal belongings? I won't spare on tips. (*When no one looks up.*) Père Gustave, start loading up the china at once. Go on!

PERE GUSTAVE (*rises uncertainly*): I haven't finished my breakfast yet. Don't look at me like that. That won't get you anywhere. (*Angry.*) You can lick my ass with your damned china! (*He sits down again.*)

SOUPEAU: Have you gone mad too? At your age? (*He looks from one person to another, then over to the motorcycle; bitterly:*) I see. You're already waiting for the Germans, are you? Has your employer reached the end of his rope? So this is the love and respect you show the man who feeds you. (*To the chauffeurs:*) I have testified for you on three differ-

ent occasions, claiming that you were indispensable
to my transport business, otherwise you would be at
the front. And this is the way you thank me. This is
the reward I get when I think I have bound my
employees to me like a little family. (*Over his shoulder.*) Simone, a cognac! I'm dizzy all of a sudden.
(*When he receives no answer:*) Simone, where are
you? — Now *she's* gone, *too!*

SIMONE *enters from the Hostelry dressed in a jacket,
ready to leave; she tries to slip past* SOUPEAU.

SOUPEAU: Simone!

SIMONE *continues on.*

SOUPEAU: Have you gone mad, not to answer me?

SIMONE *starts to run out.* SOUPEAU *shrugs his shoulders and points to his forehead.*

GEORGES: What's the matter with Simone?

SOUPEAU (*turns again toward the chauffeurs*): So you
refuse to work for me, is that it?

MAURICE: Not at all. When we've finished breakfast we'll
get underway.

SOUPEAU: And the china?

MAURICE: We'll take it along — if *you* want to load it on.

SOUPEAU: *I?*

MAURICE: Yes, you. It's yours, isn't it?

ROBERT: Of course you realize, Maurice, that we can't guarantee we'll get to Bordeaux.

SOUPEAU: This is monstrous. Do you know what will happen to you if you continue refusing to work — with the Germans almost here — you'll be shot, here, at the wall, on my orders!

Simone's parents enter from the street.

What do they want here?

MADAME MACHARD: We have come because of our Simone, Monsieur. They say the Germans are almost here and you're leaving. Simone is only a child, and Monsieur Machard is worried about the twenty francs.

SOUPEAU: She's run off. Probably to the devil.

GEORGES: Didn't she go home, Madame Machard?

MADAME MACHARD: No, Monsieur Georges.

GEORGES: That's strange.

The MAYOR *enters with two policemen.* SIMONE *hides behind them.*

SOUPEAU: You have come just in time, Philippe. (*With a large gesture.*) It seems I am faced here with a mutiny. It's time you stepped in.

MAYOR: Henri, Mademoiselle Machard has informed me that you intend to leave here with your trucks. I shall hinder this unlawful action of yours with every means at my disposal. Even if I must bring in the police. (*He motions toward the policemen.*)

SOUPEAU: Simone, did you have the nerve — ? Gentlemen, I took this creature you see here before you into my business for the good of her family!

MADAME MACHARD (*shakes* SIMONE): What have you done now?

SIMONE *is silent.*

MAURICE: I sent her.

SOUPEAU: I see! And you listened to Maurice?

MADAME MACHARD: Simone, how could you?

SIMONE: I wanted to help the Mayor, Maman. They need our trucks.

SOUPEAU: *Our* trucks!

SIMONE (*begins to grow confused*): André's roads are blocked. (*Able to go no further; to the* MAYOR:) Explain it to them, please, Monsieur.

MAYOR: Henri, you must try to conquer your selfishness. The child was right in calling me. We have no private claim to anything at a time like this. Everything we possess belongs to France. My sons are at the front the same as her brother. Which is only to say that not even our sons belong to us now!

SOUPEAU (*beside himself*): So there's no such thing as order anymore I suppose! Property rights have ceased to exist, is that it? Why don't you give my Hostelry as a gift to the Machards? Perhaps my good chauffeurs would care to go through and empty my safe? This is anarchy! May I take the liberty of reminding you, Monsieur Chavez, that Maman was at boarding school with the wife of the Prefect. And there are still telephones.

MAYOR: Henri. (*Weaker.*) I'm only doing my duty.

SOUPEAU: Philippe, be logical. You talk about what belongs to France. Do my provisions, does my priceless china, my silverware belong to anyone *but* France? Are they to fall into the hands of the Germans? Not a single cup must fall into the enemy's hands, not a single ham or a can of sardines. The enemy must be greeted by a wasteland, or have you forgotten that? You, as Mayor, ought to come to me and say: "Henri, it is your duty to rescue your possessions from the Germans." To which I of course would have to reply: "To do so, Philippe, I shall need my transport trucks."

The noise of a crowd is heard from the direction of the street. A bell rings at the front of the Hostelry and pounding is heard at the door.

SOUPEAU: What is it? Georges, go and see what it is!

GEORGES *goes into the Hostelry.*

And to my personnel here, who are so disloyal as to abandon my property, you ought to say: "Gentlemen, I call upon you as loyal Frenchmen to pack up your master's china."

GEORGES (*returns*): A horde of people from the assembly hall, Monsieur Henri. They've heard that the trucks are to be taken away. They're very disturbed and want to talk to the Mayor.

SOUPEAU (*grows pale*): There you are, Philippe. It's all Simone's doing! Hurry, Georges, close the gates.

GEORGES *goes to close the gates to the courtyard.*

Hurry, hurry! Run, why don't you! — These are the consequences of this agitation against my food bags. That mob out there! (*To the policemen:*) Do something: At once! You must call for reinforcements, Philippe, you owe me that much at least. They'll hurt me, Philippe. Help me! Please, Philippe.

MAYOR (*to the policemen*): Post yourselves at the gate. (*To* SOUPEAU:) Nonsense, nothing will happen to you. You heard him, I'm the one they want to talk to.

Pounding is heard at the courtyard gate.

Let a delegation of them in. Not more than three.

The policemen open the gate just a bit and negotiate with the crowd. Then they let in three people, TWO REFUGEES *and a* WOMAN WITH A BABY.

61

MAYOR: What is it?

ONE OF THE REFUGEES (*excitedly*): We have come to ask for the trucks now, Monsieur!

SOUPEAU: Haven't you heard the roads are to be kept clear?

WOMAN: For you? While we wait here for the German bombers?

MAYOR (*to the* REFUGEES): Madame, Messieurs, control yourselves, please. The trucks have already been secured. All Monsieur asks is to rescue a few priceless possessions from the threatening hands of the enemy.

WOMAN (*indignantly*): You see, there you are! They'd rather rescue their boxes than human beings!

An air-raid signal is heard.

VOICES FROM OUTSIDE: Stukas!

SOUPEAU: They're coming down.

The sound increases. The airplanes have dived. Everyone throws himself to the ground.

SOUPEAU (*when the planes have disappeared*): This is dangerous. I've got to get out of here.

VOICES FROM OUTSIDE: Give us the trucks! — Do you want us to be killed?

SOUPEAU: And the trucks aren't even loaded yet! Philippe!

SIMONE (*angry*): You mustn't think of your supplies now!

SOUPEAU (*dumbfounded*): How dare you talk like that, Simone?

SIMONE: But we could give the food to these people.

ONE OF THE REFUGEES: So, it's food, is it! It's food you're running off with!

MAURICE: That's the way it is.

WOMAN: And we couldn't even get soup this morning.

MAURICE: He's not rescuing his food from the Germans, he's rescuing it from the French.

WOMAN (*running back toward the gate*): Open up! Open up here!

When the policemen restrain her she calls over the wall.

Listen to me! They're loading food onto the trucks! From the Hostelry!

SOUPEAU: Philippe! You mustn't let her shout things like that!

VOICES FROM OUTSIDE: They're smuggling the food out! — Break the door down! — Aren't there any men here? — They'll take the food and make us surrender to the German tanks!

63

The REFUGEES *break down the gate. The* MAYOR *steps toward them.*

MAYOR: Messieurs, Mesdames, let there be no violence! Everything will be arranged!

While the MAYOR *deals with the* REFUGEES *at the gate, a violent battle of words ensues in the court-yard. Two main groups emerge. On one side are:* SOUPEAU, *the* REFUGEES, *the* WOMAN WITH THE BABY, *as well as Simone's parents. On the other side are:* SIMONE, MAURICE *and* ROBERT, *the* SECOND REFUGEE, PERE GUSTAVE. GEORGES *does not take sides, but continues his breakfast.*

Unnoticed, old MADAME SOUPEAU *has entered from the Hostelry. She is very old and dressed completely in black.*

WOMAN: At least eighty people here have no way of leaving.

SOUPEAU: You're taking *your* bundles with you, aren't you, Madame? Why should I leave mine behind? They're my trucks, aren't they?

MAYOR: How much room will you need, Monsieur Soupeau?

SIMONE: You know the roads, so you can wind around and leave Route 20 open for the troops.

ROBERT: I'll be damned if I'll lug his stuff through those floods of people!

SOUPEAU: Room for at least sixty boxes. Then the other truck will have room for about thirty refugees.

WOMAN: Then you want fifty of us to stay behind, is that it?

MAYOR: Let's say you'll be satisfied with half of one of the trucks. That way at least the children and the sick will be able to come along.

WOMAN: Do you want to tear our families apart!

SOUPEAU: Eight or ten more can sit on boxes. (*To* MADAME MACHARD:) I can thank your daughter for all this.

WOMAN: That child has more heart than all of you put together.

MADAME MACHARD: Please excuse our Simone, Monsieur Henri. She gets these ideas from her brother. It's terrible.

SIMONE: But you will take the sick and the children with you?

ROBERT: The refugees are something else again.

PERE GUSTAVE: Take my advice, Simone, don't get yourself mixed up in this.

SIMONE: But our beautiful France is in terrible danger, Père Gustave.

PERE GUSTAVE: She got that out of that damned book! "Is not our beautiful France in danger?"

ROBERT: Madame Soupeau has come down. She's motioning to you.

Bertolt Brecht

SIMONE *goes to* MADAME SOUPEAU.

WOMAN (*to the crowd in the gateway*): Why don't we just take the trucks and the food?

MADAME SOUPEAU: Here is the key, Simone. You may give the people whatever they want of the supplies. Père Gustave, Georges, you will help them.

MAYOR (*loudly*): Bravo, Madame Soupeau! Bravo!

SOUPEAU: Maman, how *can* you? How did you get down here? You can catch your death in this draft. And there are wines and provisions in the cellar worth seventy thousand francs.

MADAME SOUPEAU (*to the* MAYOR): They are at the disposal of the people of Saint-Martin. (*To* SOUPEAU, *coldly:*) Would you prefer to be looted?

SIMONE (*to the* WOMAN WITH THE BABY): You'll get food!

MADAME SOUPEAU: Simone! My son has agreed to your suggestion of opening the Hostelry's entire storehouse to the community. All we are concerned with now is the china and the silver, which will require very little room. Will they help us load it on?

WOMAN: And what about room on the trucks?

MADAME SOUPEAU: Madame, we will take as many of you as we are able, and the Hostelry will consider it an honor to feed all those of you left behind.

66

REFUGEE (*calling back toward the gate*): Gaston! Would the old Creveuz people and the Meinier family stay behind if they got fed?

A VOICE FROM THE BACK: Probably, Jean!

WOMAN: Wait, if we're getting fed, I'll stay, too!

MADAME SOUPEAU: You are welcome.

MAYOR (*at the gate*): Messieurs, Mesdames, help yourselves. The provisions of the Hostelry are at your disposal.

A few of the refugees go hesitantly into the supply shed.

MADAME SOUPEAU: And bring us a couple bottles of cognac, Simone, Martel '84.

SIMONE: Yes, Madame. (*She motions to the refugees and goes into the supply shed with them,* PERE GUSTAVE, *and* GEORGES.)

SOUPEAU: This will be the death of me yet, Maman.

GEORGES *and a* REFUGEE *drag out a box of food from the storehouse. The* REFUGEE *is very pleased and parodies a hawker.*

REFUGEE: Fruits, hams, chocolates, food for the trip! Free today! Free!

67

Bertolt Brecht

SOUPEAU *indignantly watches the boxes being carried by* GEORGES *and the* REFUGEE *across the courtyard toward the street entrance.*

SOUPEAU: But those are delicacies! That's foie gras!

MADAME SOUPEAU (*with restraint*): Hold your tongue! (*Courteously to the* REFUGEE:) I trust you will enjoy it, Monsieur!

The SECOND REFUGEE, *with the help of* PERE GUS-TAVE, *drags baskets of food across the courtyard.*

SOUPEAU (*indignantly*): My Pommard 1915. And my caviar. And there's my —

MAYOR: This is a time of sacrifice, Henri. (*In a choked up voice.*) It's times like this that you must show you have a heart.

MAURICE (*imitates Soupeau's outcry*): "My Pommard!" (*In the midst of resounding laughter he slaps* SIMONE *on the shoulder.*) Just to have seen this, Simone, I'll load up your boxes of china for you.

SOUPEAU (*vexed*): I don't know what there is to laugh at! (*Pointing to the disappearing boxes:*) This is robbery.

MADAME SOUPEAU: Agreed. (*She takes some of the cans of sardines and bottles of wine over to Simone's parents.*) Take some. You take some, too. And give your parents some glasses, Simone.

SIMONE *does so; then she fetches a stool, places it at*

the wall, and reaching into one of the baskets hands food over the wall to the refugees outside.

MADAME SOUPEAU: Maurice, Robert, Père Gustave, help yourselves to glasses, too. (*Indicating the policemen:*) I see the armed gentlemen are already taken care of. (*To the* WOMAN WITH THE BABY:) Have a drink with us, too, Madame. (*To all:*) Mesdames, Messieurs, let us raise our glasses to the future of our beautiful France.

SOUPEAU (*alone and shut out*): And me? Would you drink to the welfare of France without me? (*He serves himself a glass of wine and approaches the group.*)

MAYOR (*to* MADAME SOUPEAU): Madame, in the name of the people of Saint-Martin, I wish to thank the Hostelry for its generous donation. (*He lifts his glass.*) To France! To the future!

GEORGES: But where's Simone?

SIMONE *is still occupied with handing food over the wall to the refugees.*

MAYOR: Simone!

SIMONE *approaches hesitantly, perspiring.*

MADAME SOUPEAU: Yes, you take a glass, too, Simone. Each of us here is in your debt.

They all drink.

SOUPEAU (*to the chauffeurs*): Are we friends again? Do

Bertolt Brecht

you really think it didn't occur to me to use my trucks for the refugees? Maurice, Robert, I may be stubborn, but I am also able to appreciate high-minded motives when I find them. I can admit my own faults, that doesn't bother me. But you must do the same. Let's forget our little personal differences. Let us stand staunchly together against our common enemy. Let's shake hands on that!

SOUPEAU *begins with* ROBERT, *who shakes his hand with a silly smile on his face; then* GEORGES *gives him his left hand.* SOUPEAU *then puts his arm around the* WOMAN WITH THE BABY. PERE GUSTAVE *extends his hand, grumbles, still angry. Then* SOUPEAU *turns toward* MAURICE *the chauffeur.* MAURICE, *however, makes no effort to extend his hand.*

SOUPEAU: Well, well, well, are we Frenchmen or not?

SIMONE (*reproaching him*): Maurice?

MAURICE (*extends his hand hesitantly to* SOUPEAU; *ironically*): Long live our new Saint Joan, uniter of all Frenchmen.

MONSIEUR MACHARD *slaps* SIMONE *on the ear.*

MADAME MACHARD (*explaining*): That's for being forward toward Monsieur Soupeau.

SOUPEAU (*to* MONSIEUR MACHARD): No, Monsieur. (*He puts his arm around* SIMONE *consolingly.*) Simone is my darling, Madame. I have a weakness for her. (*To the chauffeurs:*) But let's start loading up now,

70

children! I'm certain even Monsieur Machard will help.

MAYOR (*to the policemen*): Lend Monsieur Soupeau a hand there.

SOUPEAU (*bows to the* WOMAN WITH THE BABY): Madame!

> *The group breaks up, and even the crowd outside disperses.* SOUPEAU, *the* MAYOR, MADAME SOUPEAU, SIMONE, MAURICE, ROBERT *and* GEORGES *remain.*

SOUPEAU: Children, I wouldn't have missed this experience for the world. The devil take my caviar and my Pommard. It's harmony I love.

MAURICE: And what about the brickyard?

MAYOR (*carefully*): He's right, Henri, something must be done about this brickyard, too.

SOUPEAU (*irritably*): What now? What more do you want from me? All right, for all I care the trucks that are out of gasoline can go to the brickyard and fill up. Are you satisfied now?

ROBERT: In Abbeville the Germans took their gasoline right out of the pumps on the street. No wonder they're so fast.

GEORGES: Our 132nd had the German tanks on their tails before they even saw them. Two of our regiments were beaten flat as a pancake.

SIMONE (*frightened*): But not the Seventh?

GEORGES: No, not the Seventh.

MAYOR: All gasoline supplies must be destroyed, Henri.

SOUPEAU: Aren't you being a bit hasty? You can't destroy everything all at once. We may even push back the enemy. Isn't that right, Simone? You tell Monsieur Chavez that France is a long way from being lost. (*To* MADAME SOUPEAU:) Good-bye, Maman. It worries me to leave you behind this way. (*Kisses her.*) But Simone will be a strong support for you. Good-bye, Simone. I'm not ashamed to thank you. You are a good Frenchman. (*Kisses her.*) As long as you're here I know that nothing will fall into German hands. Everything must be quite bare in the Hostelry, are we agreed? I know you'll do everything just as I would have. Good-bye, Philippe, my old friend. (*Puts his arms around him, takes up his baggage.* SIMONE *makes a move to help him; he motions her away.*) No, no. You talk it over with Maman and decide what should be done with the rest of our provisions. (*Goes off into the street*).

SIMONE (*running after the two chauffeurs*): Maurice, Robert! (*She kisses them both on the cheek. Then finally* MAURICE *and* ROBERT *go off.*)

VOICE OF THE RADIO ANNOUNCER: Attention! Attention! German tank formations have advanced as far as Tours. (*This announcement is repeated several times to the end of the scene.*)

MAYOR (*pale, beside himself*): Then they could even be here tonight.

MADAME SOUPEAU: Don't be an old woman, Philippe.

SIMONE: Madame, I'll run over to the brickyard with Georges and Père Gustave. We'll destroy the gasoline.

MADAME SOUPEAU: You heard Monsieur Soupeau's orders. He begged us not to do anything hasty. After all, my dear, you ought to leave something for *us* to do.

SIMONE: But, Madame, Maurice says the Germans are fast.

MADAME SOUPEAU: That will be all, Simone. (*Turns to go.*) There's a terrible draft here. (*To the* MAYOR:) I thank you, Philippe, for all you did today for the Hostelry. (*In the doorway.*) Besides, Simone, since everyone has gone I will probably be closing the Hostelry. Give me the key to the supply shed.

SIMONE, *deeply hurt, gives her the key.*

I think it were best if you went home now to your parents. I have been most satisfied with you.

SIMONE (*not understanding*): Can't I help when the people come to get the food?

MADAME SOUPEAU *goes into the Hostelry without a word.*

73

Bertolt Brecht

SIMONE (*after a silence, faltering*): Am I dismissed, Monsieur?

MAYOR (*consolingly*): I'm afraid so. But you mustn't be upset by it. You heard what she said, she was satisfied with you. Coming from her, that means a lot, Simone.

SIMONE (*tonelessly*): Yes, Monsieur.

The MAYOR *goes off dejectedly.* SIMONE *looks after him.*

(b)

THE SECOND DREAM
OF
SIMONE MACHARD

It is the night of the fifteenth of June. Confused, festive music. A group of waiting people emerges from the darkness: the MAYOR *in royal robes;* SOUPEAU *and the* COLONEL, *both in armor with a field marshal's staff in hand; the* COLONEL *wears his duster over his armor.*

COLONEL: Our dear Joan has now conquered Orléans and Rheims, after clearing Route 20 for the free advance of the troops. She must be richly rewarded, that is certain.

MAYOR: That is my concern, Monsieur, that is the King's business. The dignitaries of France and her noble families who are gathered here today shall bow to the ground before her.

From here to the end of the scene the titles and names of dignitaries and families of France are proclaimed as though they were coming to a festivity.

75

Bertolt Brecht

MAYOR: Is it true what I hear, that she has been dismissed? (*Discreetly.*) At the wish of the Queen Mother, the proud Queen Isabeau, so I've heard.

SOUPEAU: I know nothing about it, I wasn't present. I find it all most unseemly. Simone is my darling. Of course she'll stay.

The MAYOR *says something in the dream language, something apparently evasive.*

COLONEL: She's coming.

SIMONE *strides in dressed in helmet and sword, and preceded by her bodyguard consisting of* MAURICE, ROBERT, *and the soldier* GEORGES. *All three wear armor. Out of the darkness Simone's parents as well as the employees of the Hostelry and the people appear. The bodyguards keep the people back by using their spears.*

ROBERT: Make way for the Maid.

MADAME MACHARD (*straining her neck to see*): There she is. She doesn't look at all bad in that helmet.

MAYOR (*steps forward*): My dearest Joan, what can we do for you? Ask anything of us you like, at once.

SIMONE (*bowing*): First of all, Your Majesty, I would like my native town to continue being fed with the food from the Hostelry. As you know, I'm sent to

76

help the poor and the needy. The taxes must be repealed.

MAYOR: That is a matter of course. What else?

SIMONE: Second, Paris must be taken. A second campaign must begin at once, Your Majesty.

SOUPEAU (*astounded*): A second campaign?

COLONEL: What will old Madame Soupeau have to say to
that, the proud Queen Isabeau?

SIMONE: I am asking you to give me an army with which
I may completely destroy the enemy, and that before
the end of the year, Your Majesty.

MAYOR (*smiling*): Dearest Joan, we are most satisfied
with you. Coming from us, that means a lot. Let that
be enough. You must leave something for *us* to do.
I'm closing up the Hostelry now, and you are going
home. But before that, you shall be raised to the no-
bility, of course. Give me your sword, I seem to have
mislaid mine, so that I may dub you a *Grande Dame*
of France.

SIMONE (*gives him her sword and kneels down*): Here is
the key.

*The confused music laced now with the sounds of
organ and choir gives evidence of a solemn church
celebration in the distance. The* MAYOR *solemnly
touches* SIMONE's *shoulder with the sword.*

77

THE BODYGUARDS AND THE PEOPLE: Long live the Maid! Long live the *Grande Dame* of France!

SIMONE (*as the* MAYOR *begins to leave*): One moment, Your Majesty. You've forgotten to give me back my sword. (*Urgently.*) The English are still not conquered; Burgundy is assembling a new army more terrible than the first. The worst hasn't even begun.

MAYOR: Many thanks for the offer. And many thanks for all the rest, Joan (*Giving Simone's sword to* SOUPEAU.) See that it arrives safely in Bordeaux, Henri. We must now have a private talk with old Madame Soupeau, the proud Queen Isabeau. Farewell, Joan, it was a pleasure! (*He goes off with* SOUPEAU *and the* COLONEL.)

SIMONE (*terrified*): But the enemy is coming! Listen! Please!

The music dwindles to a murmur, the light grows dim, the people disappear in the darkness. SIMONE *stands there without moving, then*:

André! Help me! Come down to me, Archangel! Speak to me! The English are gathering an army, and Burgundy has deserted, and our own people are falling away.

THE ANGEL *appears on the roof of the garage.*

ANGEL (*reproachfully*): What have you done with your sword, Joan?

SIMONE (*confused, excusing herself*): They have made

me a *Grande Dame* of France but they didn't give it back to me. (*Softly, ashamed.*) I have been dismissed.

ANGEL: I understand. (*After a silence.*) Daughter of France, don't let them send you away. Be strong. France needs you. You must not yet return to your parents, for your dismissal will only serve to grieve them. You've also promised to keep your brother's job open for him in the garage; for one day he will return. Stay here, Joan. How can you desert your post now when the enemy could invade us at any moment?

SIMONE: Are we to fight even when the enemy has won?

ANGEL: Is there a breeze tonight?

SIMONE: Yes.

ANGEL: Isn't there a tree here in the yard?

SIMONE: Yes. A poplar.

ANGEL: Do its leaves rustle when the wind blows through it?

SIMONE: Yes, very clearly.

ANGEL: Then you are to fight even when the enemy has won.

SIMONE: But how am I to fight if I have no sword?

79

Bertolt Brecht

ANGEL: Listen!
When the enemy conqueror marches into your town
It must seem he has conquered nothing, all must be
down.
There must be no man left to surrender to him a key
For he who comes is no guest, he is vermin only.
Let every meal or table that he might use be abol-
ished
And every home's bedstead and every chair be de-
molished.
Whatever you cannot burn, that must be well hidden
And spilled every jug of milk and every roll buried
as bidden.
He must cry out: Help me! Be called: *Abomination!*
He must be made to eat dirt. He must live in conflag-
ration.
He must not implore any court of justice for pity.
Unrememberable, Nothing, be the name of your
once-have-been city.
Wherever he look be there nothing, wherever he
tread be it bare
So as to seem that no hostel ever existed there.
Go forth and destroy!

*The stage grows dark. Urgently, softly, again and
again, into the sound of the confused music, the
ANGEL's "Go forth and destroy!" is heard, along with
the clear rolling sound of heavy tanks.*

3

THE FIRE

(a)

Old MADAME SOUPEAU, *dressed completely in black, with* THERESE, *the chambermaid, in back of her, and* PERE GUSTAVE, *dressed in his Sunday clothes, await the* GERMAN CAPTAIN *at the gate to the courtyard.* GEORGES, *now dressed in civilian clothes, leans against the garage from which* SIMONE, *hiding from* MADAME SOUPEAU, *listens to him. The clatter of tanks rolling by is heard from outside.*

SIMONE: She's white as chalk and she's afraid.

GEORGES: She thinks they'll take her as a hostage and have her shot. She had nightmares all last night, and Thérèse heard her cry out "The butchers will murder us all!" But her greediness kept her here all the same, and now she's waiting for the German Captain. — I really don't know why you don't want her to see you, Simone. Is something wrong?

SIMONE (*lying*): No, no. Only — she'd send me away if she saw me here. She'd be afraid the Germans would hurt me.

81

Bertolt Brecht

GEORGES *(suspiciously)*: Is that the only reason she shouldn't see you?

SIMONE *(evasively)*: Do you think the Germans have caught up with Maurice and Robert?

GEORGES: Maybe. — Why did you really move out of your room in the main building, Simone?

SIMONE *(lying)*: Because there's a place now in the chauffeurs' quarters. — Do you think André will be coming back?

GEORGES: That's not very likely. — She didn't dismiss you, did she, Simone?

SIMONE *(lying)*: No.

GEORGES: The Germans are coming now.

The GERMAN CAPTAIN *enters from the street accompanied by* CAPTAIN FÉTAIN. *Polite greetings are exchanged at the courtyard gate between* MADAME SOUPEAU *and the two captains. One hears nothing of what is being said.*

GEORGES: Our good Captain Fétain, the secret Fascist, is honored to introduce the hereditary enemy to Madame. Great show of courtesy, eh? They sniff at each other and seem to find their mutual odors not unpleasant. The hereditary enemy is a gentleman, cultured and well-bred. Madame is immensely relieved. *(Whispers.)* They're coming.

82

SIMONE *steps back.* MADAME SOUPEAU *leads both gentlemen across the courtyard and into the Hostelry.* THERESE, *the chambermaid, follows.*

PERE GUSTAVE, *to whom* MADAME SOUPEAU *has whispered something, goes to* GEORGES *and* SIMONE.

PERE GUSTAVE: Madame has ordered that henceforth none of the mob from the assembly hall be allowed into the Hostelry. It might annoy the German gentleman. The way it looks now, Monsieur Soupeau could just as well have stayed here.

GEORGES: The first thing they announced over the radio was: "Those who maintain peace and order have nothing to fear."

PERE GUSTAVE: That one in there says "please" when he wants something. "Would you *please* show my orderly my rooms."

SIMONE: But he's our enemy.

PERE GUSTAVE *goes off into the supply shed.*

GEORGES: Has your cousin had another dream?

SIMONE: Yes, last night.

GEORGES: About the Maid of Orléans again?

SIMONE (*nods*): They made her a *Grande Dame.*

GEORGES: That must have been quite an experience for her.

SIMONE: And her village had its taxes repealed, just like in the book.

Bertolt Brecht

GEORGES (*somewhat sharply*): Whereas in reality the Hostelry's supplies *won't* be distributed among the villagers, as was promised.

SIMONE (*embarrassed*): My cousin didn't say anything about that.

GEORGES: Aha.

SIMONE: Monsieur Georges, when a certain person appears in a dream, like the dreams my cousin has, you know, when a person appears like an angel — does it mean that person is dead?

GEORGES: I don't think so. It only means that the little girl who dreamt those dreams was afraid that the person *might* have died. — What more does your cousin still have to do?

SIMONE: There must be an awful lot, Monsieur Georges.

GEORGES: Did anything unpleasant happen in the dream?

SIMONE: Why?

GEORGES: Because you haven't said much about it.

SIMONE (*slowly*): Nothing unpleasant happened.

GEORGES: I only asked, Simone, because I think sometimes a person can take these dreams a little too much to heart, and forget that it's bright daylight out here and not a dream.

SIMONE (*passionately*): Then I won't bother you with my cousin's dreams anymore, Monsieur!

The WOMAN WITH THE BABY *and one of the refugees from the assembly hall enter the courtyard.*

SIMONE: They're coming for the food. Tell them in a nice way, Monsieur Georges. (*She hides herself and watches.*)

GEORGES (*comes forward*): Madame.

WOMAN: The tanks are already here.

MAN: Three of them, in front of the city hall.

WOMAN: Big ones, Monsieur. Seven meters long.

MAN: (*indicating the German guards*): Careful.

MADAME SOUPEAU (*appears in the doorway of the Hostelry*): Georges! Père Gustave! Take the hors d'oeuvres into the breakfast room for the Captain! — What do you want here?

WOMAN: We've come for the food, Madame. Twenty-one of us stayed behind in the assembly hall.

MADAME SOUPEAU: I believe I made it clear to you, Georges, that the Hostelry is no longer open to beggars.

MAN: What do you mean "beggars"?

MADAME SOUPEAU: Why don't you tell these people their

85

dealings are with the German Commanders now and not with us? The good times are past.

WOMAN: And you expect us to go back to the assembly hall after you advised us to stay behind because your china needed to be loaded up?

MADAME SOUPEAU: If I were you, Madame, I would guard against becoming an informer.

WOMAN: Don't try to hide behind the Germans, Madame.

MADAME SOUPEAU (*calls back over her shoulder*): Honoré!

WOMAN: My baby and I could be with my sister in Bordeaux by this time. You promised you'd care for us, Madame.

MADAME SOUPEAU: Under compulsion, Madame.

CAPTAIN FETAIN (*stepping up behind her*): And in the wake of your pillaging! But there will be a new discipline set up here, my good people. (*Indicating the German guards:*) Shall I have you escorted out with bayonets? Don't excite yourself, Marie, think of your heart!

WOMAN: Pigs!

MAN (*restraining her and leading her off*): Our time will come, Madame.

MADAME SOUPEAU: It's beginning to smell here of dung. The sewers of the northern cities float their rats down here to our peaceful villages. These customers of cheap wine shops come to the surface just about here. This must lead to a bloody reckoning one day. Père Gustave, breakfast for four!

CAPTAIN FETAIN (*to* GEORGES): You there! The Mayor will be back here soon. Tell him I have to talk to him before he sees the German Captain.

He leads MADAME SOUPEAU *back into the Hostelry. When they have disappeared,* SIMONE *runs after the refugees.*

GEORGES: Père Gustave! The hors d'oeuvres for the German Captain!

SIMONE *returns out of breath.*

What did you say to them?

SIMONE: To tell those in the assembly hall that they'll get their food. I'll do it this evening.

GEORGES: That's right, you still have the key.

SIMONE: She promised them.

GEORGES: Just you be damned careful. This is outright thievery.

SIMONE: But Monsieur Soupeau himself said: "As long as you're here, Simone, nothing will fall into German hands, I'm sure of that."

GEORGES: But Madame says otherwise now.

SIMONE: Maybe they're forcing her.

The MAYOR *appears in the gateway.*

SIMONE *(rushes to him, whispering)*: Monsieur, what's going to happen?

MAYOR: What do you think, Simone? I have some good news for you! I've proposed that your father be appointed a bailiff. You earned that, Simone. Now having lost your job doesn't matter so much.

SIMONE *(whispering)*: Monsieur, is it true there are three tanks in front of the city hall? *(Even more softly.)* The gasoline is still here.

MAYOR *(distractedly)*: Yes, that's bad. *(Suddenly.)* By the way, what are you doing here, Simone?

SIMONE: But something *has* to be done with the gasoline, Monsieur! Can't *you* do anything? They're sure to ask Madame Soupeau about it.

MAYOR: I don't think we need worry ourselves about Madame Soupeau, Simone.

SIMONE: I could do something. I know my way around the brickyard.

MAYOR *(fearfully)*: I hope you're intending nothing rash, Simone. You must understand, I have a tremendous responsibility toward the people of Saint-Martin.

SIMONE: Yes, Monsieur.

MAYOR: I don't know why I'm talking to you like this, Simone, you're still a child. But I do think that everyone should do his best now, don't you?

SIMONE: Yes, Monsieur. If the brickyard just happens to burn down ...

MAYOR: For the love of God, Simone! You mustn't even think such a thing. But now I have to go inside. This is the most difficult step I have ever taken in all my life. (*He starts to go in.*)

CAPTAIN FETAIN *comes out.*

CAPTAIN FETAIN: Monsieur Chavez. You're just in time for breakfast.

MAYOR: I have had my breakfast.

CAPTAIN FETAIN: That is regretable. You seem not to be properly informed. And then yesterday all sorts of unpleasant things happened, and that with the express indulgence of the authorities. I find it most lamentable that certain elements, who are not above exploiting the collapse of France for their own private ends, were not immediately subdued. Our German guests might well expect a gesture of courtesy from us. The German Commander, for example, has already been informed of a certain commodity stored in a brickyard. Perhaps you can adapt yourself to the situation, Chavez. And perhaps you might work up an appetite. After you, Monsieur.

MAYOR (*very unsurely*): After you, Captain.

Bertolt Brecht

Both gentlemen go into the Hostelry. PERE GUSTAVE, *entering from the supply shed, follows them.*

PERE GUSTAVE (*going in with the delicacies*): Calm seas and prosperous voyage! The rich will always flock with the rich, eh, Georges? They sell out France like they do their delicacies! (*He goes off.*)

SIMONE *has paid close attention. She has seated herself.*

GEORGES: Simone! What's the matter with you? Simone?

SIMONE *does not answer him.* GEORGES *remains in the position of trying to rouse her. During* SIMONE's *daydream we hear the weak and mechanical repetition of* PERE GUSTAVE's: *"The rich will always flock with the rich."*

(b)

THE DAYDREAM
OF
SIMONE MACHARD

The twentieth of June. Confused war music. The back wall of the Hostelry becomes transparent. Playing scat on a marble table in front of a gigantic Gobelin tapestry are the MAYOR *as* KING CHARLES VII, CAPTAIN FETAIN *as the* DUKE OF BURGUNDY, *the* GERMAN CAPTAIN, *his sword across his knees, and* MADAME SOUPEAU *as the* QUEEN MOTHER ISABEAU.

MADAME-ISABEAU: I wish to see nothing more of the mob, Milord.

GERMAN CAPTAIN-MILORD: You may hide yourself behind us, Queen Isabeau. I'll have them cleared from the courtyard, then we shall have some order here. — I win.

MAYOR-KING: Listen! Do I hear the sound of a drum on the breeze?

The sounds of Joan's drum are heard in the distance.

CAPTAIN FETAIN-BURGUNDY: I don't hear anything. — Lay out your ace.

The drumming stops.

MAYOR-KING (*doubtful*): Are you sure? I have a premonition, Burgundy, that my Joan has fallen into danger and needs our help!

CAPTAIN FETAIN-BURGUNDY: Ten of hearts. — How can I take care of my wine business properly with the war on?

GERMAN CAPTAIN-MILORD: How much are your delicacies, Madame?

MADAME-ISABEAU: Whose deal? — Ten thousand pieces of silver, Milord.

MAYOR-KING: But this time I'm sure of it. She is definitely in danger, in mortal danger. I must go to her rescue and destroy everything. (*He rises, cards in hand.*)

CAPTAIN FETAIN-BURGUNDY: Beware. If you leave now it will be the last time. You are not properly informed. How do you expect us to play with all these interruptions? — Jack.

MAYOR-KING (*sits down again*): Well, all right.

MADAME-ISABEAU (*gives him a slap on the ear*): That's for being forward.

GERMAN CAPTAIN-MILORD: Permit me, Queen Isabeau.

(*He counts out gold pieces onto the table.*) One, two, three . . .

GEORGES *shakes* SIMONE *out of her daydream while the* GERMAN CAPTAIN *continues counting.*

GEORGES: Simone! You're daydreaming now with your eyes wide open.

SIMONE: Are you coming with me, Monsieur Georges?

GEORGES (*staring at his bandaged arm; happily*): Simone, I can move it again.

SIMONE: I'm so glad, Monsieur. But we must get to the brickyard. There isn't much time. You must come, too, Père Gustave, quick.

PERE GUSTAVE (*coming out of the Hostelry*): Me? They've just nailed up a poster saying that whoever destroys usable war supplies will be shot. They're dead serious, these people.

SIMONE: The Mayor *wants* us to do it.

PERE GUSTAVE: The Mayor's an asshole.

SIMONE: But *you're* coming, Monsieur Georges? It's for André. I have no idea how to destroy so much gasoline. Do I have to burn the whole brickyard?

GEORGES: Don't you understand: I can move it again.

SIMONE (*looks at them*): Then you don't want to come with me?

93

PERE GUSTAVE: There's another one of those.

> *A* GERMAN SOLDIER *enters the courtyard carrying the baggage.* SIMONE, *as soon as she sees him, rushes away frightened.*

> *The* GERMAN SOLDIER *throws down the baggage and, perspiring, airs his steel helmet; he starts in a friendly manner to make himself understood through gestures.*

GERMAN SOLDIER: Captain? Inside?

GEORGES (*with gestures*): There. In the Hostelry. Cigarette?

GERMAN SOLDIER (*takes a cigarette and grins*): War — shit.

> *He makes a gesture to indicate shooting, then a contemptuous movement of the hand.*

GEORGES (*laughing*): Bum bum. (*He makes a farting sound with his lips, then both of them laugh.*)

GERMAN SOLDIER: Captain — asshole.

GEORGES: What? What's that?

GERMAN SOLDIER (*imitates the* GERMAN CAPTAIN *with a monocle*): *Merde.*

GEORGES (*understands, then happily mimics* MADAME SOUPEAU *and* CAPTAIN FETAIN): They're all *merde.* All shit.

They laugh again, then the GERMAN SOLDIER *takes up the baggage and goes inside.*

GEORGES (*to* PERE GUSTAVE): My-my-my, how easy it could be to understand each other.

PERE GUSTAVE: You'd better be careful.

GEORGES: And how. Now that my arm's getting better.

Out of the Hostelry come the GERMAN CAPTAIN, CAPTAIN FETAIN, *the* MAYOR, *and* MADAME SOUPEAU.

CAPTAIN FETAIN: I consider myself fortunate, Captain, that we were able to come to so intimate an understanding.

GERMAN CAPTAIN: I thank you, Madame, for placing the gasoline supply so spontaneously at our disposal. Not that the army needs it, of course. However, we will accept it as a token of your spirit of collaboration.

MADAME SOUPEAU: The brickyard is not far.

GERMAN CAPTAIN: I'll send my tanks there.

The sky has grown red. The group stands there, stupefied. Distant explosions.

GERMAN CAPTAIN: What's that?

CAPTAIN FETAIN (*hoarsely*): The brickyard.

(c)

Night. Pounding is heard at the courtyard gate. GEORGES *comes out of his room and opens the gate to* SOUPEAU *and the two chauffeurs.*

SOUPEAU: How are you, Georges? Is Maman all right? The Hostelry seems to be still standing. I feel like after the Flood. How are you, Simone?

SIMONE enters, half-dressed, from the chauffeurs' quarters. ROBERT *embraces her.* PERE GUSTAVE *has also appeared.*

ROBERT: What do you mean, setting yourself up in our rooms! (*He dances around with her, humming.*)
Bloody Jack came back, came back
His Rosie was still here
And Maman had a small Chartreuse
And Papa had a beer.

SOUPEAU: Anything new happen?

GEORGES: We have a German Captain living here. Madame Soupeau's a bit exhausted because of the brickyard investigation. The German Captain . . .

SOUPEAU: The *what* investigation?

SIMONE: Monsieur Henri, we did everything just as you would have. I even took food to the assembly hall yesterday evening.

SOUPEAU: I want to know what has happened to the brickyard.

96

GEORGES (*hesitantly*): It burned to the ground, Monsieur Henri.

SOUPEAU: Burned to the ground? — The Germans?

GEORGES *shakes his head.*

Carelessness? (*He looks from one to the other. No one answers.*) The authorities?

GEORGES: No.

SOUPEAU: The rabble from the assembly hall?

GEORGES: No, Monsieur Henri.

SOUPEAU: Then it was arson. (*Bellowing as though his foot were cut off.*) Who? (*No answer.*) So, it's a conspiracy, is it? (*In a cold rage.*) You've become criminals at last. But that was to be expected after the proof you showed me of your gratitude the day I left. "Lick my ass with your damned china!" eh? All right, I accept your challenge. Just you wait and see.

GEORGES: It was because of the Germans, Monsieur Henri.

SOUPEAU (*sarcastically*): Oh, I see, it happens to be *my* brickyard but you burned it because of the Germans. Well, in your hate and destructiveness you were blind enough to cut off the hand that fed you. (*Abruptly.*) Simone!

SIMONE: Yes, Monsieur.

SOUPEAU: I want to know here and now who is responsible for this.

SIMONE: I am, Monsieur.

SOUPEAU: What? You had the nerve to — ? (*Pulling her by the arm.*) Who made you do it? Who was behind it?

SIMONE: No one, Monsieur.

SOUPEAU: Don't lie, you hear! I won't tolerate —

GEORGES: Please, leave her alone, Monsieur. She's not lying.

SOUPEAU: Who ordered you to do it?

SIMONE: I did it for my brother, Monsieur.

SOUPEAU: Ah, André! He was the one who incited you against me, was he? "We, the masses," eh? I always knew he was a Red. Who *helped* you do it?

SIMONE: No one, Monsieur.

SOUPEAU: And *why* did you do it?

SIMONE: Because of the gasoline, Monsieur.

SOUPEAU: And for that you had to burn the whole brick-yard? Why couldn't you have let it run out into a sewer?

SIMONE: I didn't know, Monsieur Henri.

GEORGES: She's only a child, Monsieur Henri.

SOUPEAU: Arsonists! All of you! Robbers! Get out of here, Père Gustave! You're dismissed, Georges! You're worse than Germans.

GEORGES: Very well, Monsieur Henri.

He stands beside SIMONE.

SOUPEAU: Who said something about an investigation? What's it about?

GEORGES: The Germans are investigating the fire.

SOUPEAU: Then it happened while the Germans were here.

GEORGES: Yes.

SOUPEAU (*having to sit down; in despair*): That too, now! The Hostelry ruined! (*Supports his hand in his hands.*)

PERE GUSTAVE: Monsieur Henri, the people of Saint-Martin spoke very highly about the Hostelry yesterday afternoon. "They did it right under the noses of the Germans," they said.

SOUPEAU: I'll be court-martialed. And you've brought me to this. (*In despair.*) I'll be shot.

SIMONE (*steps forward*): They won't shoot you, Monsieur, since I was the one who did it. You can go with me to the German Captain, and I'll take the blame for everything, Monsieur.

Bertolt Brecht

MAURICE: That's out of the question.

SOUPEAU: Why is it out of the question? She's a child. They wouldn't dare touch her.

MAURICE: You can tell the Germans it was Simone, if you like, but we're going to get her out of here. Get dressed, Simone, at once.

SOUPEAU: Then that makes us accomplices.

SIMONE: Maurice, I have to stay. André wants me to, I know he does.

SOUPEAU: It all depends on whether she did it *after* the Germans arrived or *before*. If she did it before, then it is an act of war, and they can't touch her.

PERE GUSTAVE (*fawningly:*) As soon as they arrived, Monsieur Henri, they nailed up a poster that said anyone responsible for an unfriendly action would be shot.

SOUPEAU (*to* SIMONE): Did you see the poster?

SIMONE: Yes, Monsieur Henri.

SOUPEAU: What did it look like?

SIMONE: It was on red paper.

SOUPEAU: Is that right?

PERE GUSTAVE *nods.*

100

And now for the questions the Germans will ask you, Simone. Did you read it *after* you set fire to the brickyard? If so, then there was no sabotage involved, Simone, and they can't do anything to you.

SIMONE: I read it before, Monsieur.

SOUPEAU: I don't think you understood me. If you read the poster *afterward,* the Germans will probably only place you in custody of the Mayor, because then your action will concern only the French, and you'll be free, Simone. Do you understand?

SIMONE: Yes, Monsieur. But I read it before.

SOUPEAU: She's confused. Père Gustave, you were in the courtyard at the time. When did Simone leave?

PERE GUSTAVE: Before, Monsieur Henri, naturally before they put up the poster.

SOUPEAU: There, you see?

SIMONE: You're making a mistake, Père Gustave. You said to me yourself before I went away that the poster forbade me to do it.

PERE GUSTAVE: I said nothing of the sort.

SOUPEAU: Of course not.

MAURICE: Can't you see, Monsieur Henri, that this child wants none of your tricks? She's not ashamed of what she did.

101

SIMONE: Monsieur Soupeau only wants to help me, Maurice.

SOUPEAU: That's right. You trust me, don't you, Simone? Then listen carefully. The men we are going to be speaking with now are the enemy. That makes a great difference, you understand. He's going to ask you a lot of questions, but you will only answer what will be for the good of Saint-Martin and France. That's simple enough, isn't it?

SIMONE: Yes, Monsieur, but I want to say nothing that isn't true.

SOUPEAU: I understand. You want to say nothing that isn't true. Not even to the enemy. Good. I accept that. I beg you now for only one thing: tell them nothing; leave that to us. Leave that to me. (*Almost in tears.*) I'll stand behind you to the end, you know that. We all stand behind you. We are Frenchmen.

SIMONE: Yes, Monsieur.

SOUPEAU *takes* SIMONE *by the hand and leads her into the Hostelry.*

MAURICE: She should have read her book more carefully.

4

THE TRIAL

(a)

THE FOURTH DREAM OF
SIMONE MACHARD

The night of the twenty-first of June. Confused music.
SIMONE *dressed as the Maid of Orléans and the* GERMAN
CAPTAIN *dressed in armor are found standing in the court-*
yard; she is surrounded by soldiers dressed in black scaly
armor with red swastikas; one of the soldiers, recognizable
as the German Captain's Orderly, holds a standard with
a swastika on its flag.

GERMAN CAPTAIN: We have you now, Joan of Orléans,
    and you will be delivered up to a high court which
    will decide why you are to be sentenced to die at
    the stake.

All go off with the exception of SIMONE *and the*
STANDARD-BEARER.

SIMONE: What kind of court is this?

STANDARD-BEARER: No ordinary one. It's an ecclesiastical
    court.

Bertolt Brecht

SIMONE: I confess to nothing.

STANDARD-BEARER: That's all well and good, but the trial seems to be over already.

SIMONE: Do you mean they sentence people before they've even heard them?

STANDARD-BEARER: Yes. Of course.

People emerge from the Hostelry who appear to have been present at the trial. They cross the courtyard and go into the street.

PERE GUSTAVE (*while crossing the courtyard, to* THERESE): Sentenced to death! And at her age!

THERESE: Yes, who would have thought it, even the day before yesterday!

SIMONE (*tugging at her sleeve*): Is Hitler here himself?

THERESE *seems not to notice her, goes off with* PERE GUSTAVE. *Simone's parents cross the courtyard, her father in uniform, her mother in black.*

MADAME MACHARD (*sobbing*): She was headstrong even when only a little child. Just like her brother. It's a terrible blow for Monsieur Machard. And with him a bailiff now, too! It's a disgrace! (*Both go off.*)

The brothers MAURICE *and* ROBERT PRIEUX *cross the courtyard.*

ROBERT: She didn't look at all bad.

MAURICE: Especially in the blue with the frills.

SIMONE (*tugs* ROBERT *by the sleeve*): Did you see the court?

ROBERT (*casually*): Yes, of course.

SIMONE: Will I see it too?

ROBERT: Undoubtedly. The judges will be coming out to break the staff over you. It's the sign that you've been condemned to death. (*Both go off.*)

A LOUD VOICE: Silence! Make way there! The condemnation of the Maid will now take place. Presiding is the High Ecclesiastical Court of the Reverend Bishops and Cardinals of Rouen. The staff will first be broken over the Maid.

A judge dressed in the splendid garb of a cardinal enters from the entrance to the Hostelry. He holds a breviary in front of his face so as not to be recognized, and crosses the courtyard. He stops in front of a bronze tripod, turns away, closes his breviary, removes a small staff from his sleeve, breaks it solemnly and tosses the broken pieces into the brazier.

A LOUD VOICE: His Eminence, the Bishop of Beauvais. For the liberation of the Orléans: Death.

Before continuing on he calmly turns his head back over his shoulder. He is the COLONEL.

SIMONE: Colonel! Monsieur!

A second judge enters from the entrance to the Hostelry and performs the same ceremony.

A LOUD VOICE: For the liberation of the City of Orléans and because the rats of the City of Orléans were fed — with stolen food: Death.

The second judge, too, shows his face. He is CAPTAIN FETAIN.

SIMONE: Captain Fétain! Monsieur!

A third judge enters from the entrance to the Hostelry and performs the same ceremony.

A LOUD VOICE: For the plot against the City of Paris and for the illegal gasoline: Death.

The third judge is SOUPEAU.

SIMONE: But, Monsieur Henri, it's me, it's me you're condemning.

SOUPEAU *performs his gesture of helplessness, and a fourth judge enters from the entrance to the Hostelry and performs the same ceremony.*

A LOUD VOICE: For the unification of all Frenchmen: Death.

The fourth judge holds his breviary in too cramped a manner so that it falls from his hands. He bends down hastily to pick it up and is seen to be the MAYOR.

SIMONE: The Mayor! Oh, Monsieur Chavez!

A LOUD VOICE: Your High Judges have spoken, Joan.

SIMONE: But they are all Frenchmen. (*To the* STANDARD-BEARER:) It's a mistake!

STANDARD-BEARER: No, Mademoiselle, the Court of Justice is French.

The four judges have stopped in the courtyard entrance.

MAYOR: You should know that from your book. Naturally the Maid is condemned by French judges, that's as it should be since she herself is French.

SIMONE (*confused*): That's true. That I'm to be condemned to die I know from my book. But I would like to know why. You see, I could never quite understand why.

MAYOR (*to the judges*): She wants a trial.

CAPTAIN FETAIN: What's the sense of having a trial when the sentence has already been pronounced?

MAYOR: Well, then at least we'll have had an investigation, we'll have heard the accused, argued the matter and weighed it in the balance.

COLONEL: And found her wanting. (*Shrugs his shoulder.*) But all right, if you demand it.

SOUPEAU: Of course we're not prepared for this.

*They put their heads together in a whispering con-
clave.* PERE GUSTAVE *brings out a table and sets it
with plates and candles. The judges seat themselves
around the table.*

PERE GUSTAVE: The refugees from the assembly hall are
outside. They want to be admitted to the trial.

SOUPEAU: Impossible, I'm expecting Maman; she says
that they stink.

CAPTAIN FETAIN (*toward the back*): The trial will take
place behind closed doors. In the interest of the State.

SOUPEAU: Where are the records? Probably mislaid, like
everything else here.

MAYOR: Where is the plaintiff?

The judges look at one another.

Well, it isn't official without a plaintiff.

SOUPEAU: Père Gustave: a plaintiff from the supply shed.

PERE GUSTAVE (*stands in the courtyard gate and calls out
in the direction of the street*): The High Ecclesiastical Court of Rouen summons a person with complaints against the Maid to come forward. — No
one? (*He repeats the summons.*) The High Ecclesiastical Court of Rouen summons a person with complaints against the Maid to come forward. (*To the
judges:*) A plaintiff! The Queen Mother Isabeau,
partisan of the renegade the Duke of Burgundy and
the hereditary enemy.

MADAME SOUPEAU *enters in battle armor from the Hostelry. She greets the judges who bow deeply to her, and officiates with the routine amiableness of the mistress of a large hostelry.*

MADAME SOUPEAU: Good evening, Captain Fétain. Keep your seat. Don't let me disturb you. (*Over her shoulder into the Hostelry.*) One Alsace-Lorraine for Captain Fétain, well done. How would you like the peasants, Constable? Are you satisfied with the service this time, Colonel? (*Indicating* SIMONE.) Everything would have been saved if this Maid of Orléans hadn't upset the proceedings. Who's to decide here, the Church or the servants of the Hostelry? (*Begins to scream as though she were mad.*) I insist that this individual be executed at once for heresy and insubordination as well as for her forward behavior. Heads must roll. Blood must flow. She must be bloodily exterminated. We must make a bloody example of her for all to see. (*Exhausted.*) My drops, Honoré.

CAPTAIN FETAIN: A chair here for the Queen Mother.

PERE GUSTAVE *brings her a chair.*

SOUPEAU: Aren't you uncomfortable in this armor, Maman? Why are you in battle dress?

MADAME SOUPEAU: I'm engaged in a war, too.

SOUPEAU: What kind of war is it?

MADAME SOUPEAU: My own war. Against that seditious Maid who incited the refugees at the assembly hall.

CAPTAIN FETAIN (*sharply*): Pst! (*To* SIMONE:) With what right did you lead these Frenchmen into war, Joan?

SIMONE: An Angel commanded me to do so, most Reverend Bishop of Beauvais.

The judges look at one another.

SOUPEAU: An angel, you say? What kind of angel?

SIMONE: From the village church. The one to the left of the altar.

CAPTAIN FETAIN: Never saw it.

MAYOR (*in a friendly way*): What did this angel look like, Simone? Describe him to us.

SIMONE: He was very young and had a beautiful voice, worthy gentlemen. He said I was to —

COLONEL (*interrupting*): What he said doesn't concern us here. In what dialect did he speak? Like an educated man? Or otherwise?

SIMONE: I don't know. Just like everybody speaks.

CAPTAIN FETAIN: Aha.

SOUPEAU: Well then, how was this angel dressed?

SIMONE: He was very beautifully dressed. His clothes were made of material that costs us twenty to thirty francs a meter in Tours.

CAPTAIN FETAIN: Do I understand you correctly, Simone,

otherwise known as Joan, that your angel was not one of those great and splendid angels whose clothes cost perhaps between two hundred and three hundred francs per meter?

SIMONE: I don't know.

COLONEL: In what condition were his clothes? Quite threadbare?

SIMONE: The Angel was just a little bit crumbled away, at the sleeve.

COLONEL: Aha. Crumbled away at the sleeve. As though he had worn his clothes to work, too, is that right? Torn perhaps?

SIMONE: No, not torn.

CAPTAIN FETAIN: Yes, of course, crumbled away. And where you say he was crumbled away, it isn't impossible, is it, that his sleeve might have become torn while working? Perhaps you failed to notice it because the color had crumbled away. But it is possible, isn't it?

SIMONE *is silent.*

COLONEL: Did this angel at any time say anything which might have been said by a person of rank? Consider that well.

SIMONE: He spoke more in general.

MAYOR: Did the angel resemble anyone you might know?

Bertolt Brecht

SIMONE (*softly*): My brother André.

COLONEL: The private soldier André Machard! My Lords, there you have your answer. A most remarkable angel, you must admit.

MADAME SOUPEAU: A veritable angel of the wine pubs, a gutter-Gabriel! In any case we know now where these "voices" of hers came from. From wine shops and privy pits.

SIMONE: You have no right to abuse the Angel, most Reverend Bishops and Cardinals.

SOUPEAU: On page one hundred and twenty-four of your book you will find that we are an Ecclesiastical Court, which is to say, the highest authority upon earth.

COLONEL: Don't you think that we, as Emminent Cardinals of the Church and of France, have a clearer conception of what is the Will of God than any tramp of an angel who might happen by?

CAPTAIN FETAIN: Where is God, Joan? Up or down? And where did your so-called angel come from? From down there! And therefore whose emissary is he? God's? Or perhaps the devil's?

MADAME SOUPEAU: The devil's! Joan of Orléans, the voices you have heard are from the devil!

SIMONE (*loudly*): No! No! They're *not* from the devil!

CAPTAIN FETAIN: Then why don't you call him, this angel

of yours? Perhaps he'll defend you, the great Maid of Orléans. Bailiff, do your duty.

PERE GUSTAVE (*calls out*): The High Ecclesiastical Court of Rouen summons the Angel of the Unknown Name, and said to have appeared to the Maid on numerous nights, to give testimony before this Court.

SIMONE *looks toward the roof of the garage. It remains empty.* PERE GUSTAVE *repeats the summons.*

(*Calls out*): The High Ecclesiastical Court of Rouen summons the Angel of the Unknown Name, and said to have appeared to the Maid on numerous nights, to give testimony before this Court.

SIMONE, *in great distress, looks at the smiling judges. Then she crouches down and in great confusion begins to beat upon the earth as though it were an unseen drum. Still, one hears nothing, and the roof of the garage remains empty.*

SIMONE: It doesn't sound here. What's happened? Why doesn't it sound? The earth of France doesn't sound anymore! It doesn't sound here!

MADAME SOUPEAU (*goes toward her*): You don't even know who France is!

(b)

The morning of the twenty-second of June. A French flag, with mourning crepe, hangs at half-mast from the archway. GEORGES, ROBERT, *and* PERE GUSTAVE *listen as* MAURICE *reads from a black-rimmed newspaper.*

MAURICE: The Marshal says that the articles of the armistice will not impair the honor of France.

PERE GUSTAVE: That's a consolation.

MAURICE: Certainly. The Marshal continues that the people of France have only to gather round him as a father. We need new discipline and order.

PERE GUSTAVE: That's the way it is. André's not fighting anymore, they've laid down his weapons for him. He'll have to be taught strict discipline now.

GEORGES: It's a good thing Simone isn't here.

Out of the Hostelry comes the GERMAN CAPTAIN *without a hat on and with a sword belt in his hand. He smokes a breakfast cigar. He looks the people over indifferently and saunters toward the gate. He looks out for awhile, then turns and goes quickly into the Hostelry.*

PERE GUSTAVE: He didn't like it from the start that all all this was a child's fault.

GEORGES: I can't understand why she ran off. She always wanted to stay no matter what. Something must have

114

frightened her. She simply crawled through the window of the laundry room.

SOUPEAU *enters from the Hostelry, rubbing his hands.*

SOUPEAU: Maurice, Robert! Unload the boxes with the china and silverware! (*More softly after he has looked around.*) I won't ask you whether or not any of my employees was involved in a certain escape of last night. What's done is done, and I'll go as far as to say that maybe it wasn't the worst of solutions. Not that there was ever any real danger. The Germans aren't cannibals, and I know how to handle them. I said this morning at breakfast to the German Captain: "It's a farce! Before the poster, after the poster, what's the sense of it all! She's just a child! What can you expect! So she's a little weak-minded, perhaps, maybe even a psychopathic case! The tanks! They must be stopped, destroy everything! And matches, of course, that's always capital fun. A political plot? A child's prank!"

GEORGES (*looking at the others*): Just what do you mean, Monsieur Henri, a child's prank?

SOUPEAU: I said the same thing to Maman: She's a child!

GEORGES: That child was the only person in this Hostelry who carried out her duties; nobody besides her lifted a finger. And Saint-Martin won't forget that, Monsieur Henri.

SOUPEAU (*out of humor*): Just do your own duty and un-

115

load the boxes. I consider it fortunate that the matter is closed. I'm convinced that the German Captain will not look too long for Simone. And now to your work! That's what our poor France needs right now! (*He goes off.*)

GEORGES: Everything's eased up all along the line: because she's gone!

MAURICE: And it hadn't the least thing to do with patriotism and the like! That would have been unpleasant. "The Germans aren't cannibals." One was just about to make a nice gesture and give the gasoline to the Germans that they'd kept back from their own army, and then the rabble interferes and they call it patriotic.

The MAYOR enters through the courtyard gate. He is pale and returns no one's greeting as he goes into the Hostelry.

MAYOR (*turning around*): Are they guarding the door to Madame Soupeau's room?

PERE GUSTAVE: No, Monsieur Chavez.

The MAYOR goes off.

PERE GUSTAVE: He's probably here because the Germans want the assembly hall cleared. It wouldn't surprise me if it's all Madame Soupeau's doing!

ROBERT: The new discipline and order!

116

PERE GUSTAVE: As far as Simone is concerned, Maurice, it'll have to be ordinary arson, because the insurance company will have to pay off the damages. They don't forget things like that too easily.

SIMONE *enters through the courtyard gate between two German soldiers with bayonets on their weapons.*

GEORGES: Simone! What happened?

SIMONE (*unmoving, very pale*): I was still at the assembly hall.

ROBERT: You mustn't be afraid. The Germans won't hurt you.

SIMONE: They said at the inquest yesterday evening that they would turn me over to the French authorities, Robert.

GEORGES: Why did you run away?

SIMONE *does not answer. The soldiers shove her into the Hostelry.*

MAURICE: So the matter is by no means settled for the Germans. Monsieur Henri is mistaken.

MADAME MACHARD *and* MONSIEUR MACHARD *enter through the courtyard gate, the latter dressed in his bailiff's uniform.*

MADAME MACHARD: Have they brought her in yet? This is terrible. Monsieur Machard is beside himself. It

117

isn't just that the payment on our farm lease is due; what eats at Monsieur Machard is the shame of it. I always knew that it would end this way, this constant book reading drove her out of her mind. And then at seven this morning there was a knock at the door and the Germans standing in the yard. "Messieurs," I said, "if you can't find our daughter, then she must have killed herself. Fire or no fire, she would never have deserted the Hostelry otherwise. If only for her brother's sake."

SOUPEAU *enters from the Hostelry.*

SOUPEAU: It's too much, Madame Machard, it's too much! She has cost me one hundred thousand francs. Not counting the wear on my nerves.

MADAME SOUPEAU *enters from the Hostelry. She has a firm grip on* SIMONE's *arm and leads her across the courtyard into the supply shed.* SIMONE *is hesitant. Behind them follow the* MAYOR *and* CAPTAIN FETAIN. *The four go into the shed. Those in the courtyard look on with amazement.*

MAYOR (*in the doorway of the shed*): Machard, I want you to go over to the assembly hall and see that the evacuation is peaceably carried out. Explain to them that the Germans need the rooms. (*Goes off into the shed.*)

MADAME MACHARD: Of course, Monsieur.

Both MACHARDS *leave with an air of dignity.*

ROBERT: What do they want with her in the shed? What are they doing to her, Monsieur Henri?

SOUPEAU: Don't ask so many questions. Our responsibilities are immeasurable now. One false step and the Hostelry's undone.

MADAME SOUPEAU *returns from the shed with* SIMONE, *behind her are the* MAYOR *and* CAPTAIN FETAIN.

MADAME SOUPEAU: I believe, Monsieur Chavez, that I have convinced you with my evidence that this girl allowed my cellar, full of supplies and fifty thousand francs of my best wine, to remain unlocked. How many other cases were lost as a result I can only guess at. In order the better to deceive me, she gave me the key in your presence. (*Turns to* SIMONE.) It has come to my attention, Simone, that you personally took whole baskets of food to the assembly hall. What did you get for it? Where is the money?

SIMONE: I took no money for it, Madame.

MADAME SOUPEAU: Don't lie. That isn't all that happened. The morning on which Monsieur Henri left here, he was threatened by the rabble because a rumor had been spread that our delivery trucks were to be driven away. Did you spread this rumor?

SIMONE: I told it to the Mayor, Madame.

MADAME SOUPEAU: Who else was in his office when you told him? Refugees?

119

SIMONE: Yes, I think so.

MADAME SOUPEAU: Oh, you think so. And when the mob arrived here, what did you tell them in regard to the supplies of the Hostelry that had employed you?

SIMONE *does not understand.*

Did you or did you not tell them to take whatever they wanted?

SIMONE: I don't remember anymore, Madame.

MADAME SOUPEAU: I see.

MAYOR: What are you trying to prove, Madame?

MADAME SOUPEAU: Who were the first to receive any of the supplies, Simone? Quite right, your parents. They helped themselves quite handsomely.

ROBERT: This has gone too far. (*To* MADAME SOUPEAU:) You forced the cans on them yourself.

GEORGES (*simultaneously*): You yourself put the supplies at the Mayor's disposal.

MAYOR: He's right, Madame.

MADAME SOUPEAU (*unswervingly to* SIMONE): You have proven yourself to be impertinent, disloyal, and forward. And that is the very reason why I dismissed you. Did you leave the Hostelry as I ordered you?

SIMONE: No, Madame.

MADAME SOUPEAU: No; instead you stayed around here, and then out of vengeance for your dismissal you set fire to the brickyard. Didn't you?

SIMONE (*excited*): But I did it because of the Germans.

ROBERT: All Saint-Martin knows that.

MADAME SOUPEAU: Oh? Because of the Germans? And who informed you that the Germans would even learn of the gasoline?

SIMONE: I heard Captain Fétain tell the Mayor.

MADAME SOUPEAU: So you heard that we were going to declare the gasoline?

SIMONE: Captain Fétain was going to.

MADAME SOUPEAU: Then you burned the gasoline only so that we could not give it to them. That is precisely what I wanted to make clear.

SIMONE (*in despair*): I did it against the enemy! There were three tanks in front of the city hall.

MADAME SOUPEAU: And *they* were the enemy? Or was it perhaps someone *else*?

Two Gray Ladies, accompanied by a POLICEMAN, *appear at the entrance to the courtyard.*

121

MAYOR: What is it, Jules?

POLICEMAN: These Ladies are from the reformatory, the Gray House.

CAPTAIN FETAIN: I telephoned the Gray House in your name, Chavez. (*To the Gray Ladies*:) This is the Machard girl, Ladies.

MAYOR: What right did you have — ?

CAPTAIN FETAIN: You can't possibly consider permitting this girl to run free, Monsieur. (*Sharply.*) The least our guests can expect of us is that we purge Saint-Martin of all dangerous elements. You appear not to have studied the honorable Marshal's address. France will go through a time of danger. It is our duty once and for all to exterminate these germs of insubordination which have proven so contagious. One fire in Saint-Martin is sufficient, Chavez.

MAURICE: I see. We do the dirty work for the Germans, eh? And then we're happy to have been of service, is that it?

MADAME SOUPEAU (*coldly*): I shall of course apply to the State Prosecutor's office in Tours for the authority to hand over the Machard girl to the Ladies of the Gray House. Simone deliberately set fire to the brickyard, the property of the Hostelry, for purely personal motives.

GEORGES: Simone and personal motives!

122

MAYOR (*shaken*): Are you trying to ruin this child?

ROBERT (*threateningly*): Who's the vengeful one now?

SOUPEAU: Don't start that again, Robert. She's still a minor. She will be placed under the protection of the Gray Ladies of the reformatory.

MAURICE (*horrified*): In that flogging-house?

SIMONE (*cries out*): No!

MAYOR: Simone in an institution for the feeble-minded! For the feeble-minded! In that house of mental torture, in that hell! Don't you realize you're sending her to her death?

MAURICE (*pointing to the Ladies with the brutal faces*): Take a look at them!

The faces of the Ladies remain unmoving and mask-like.

GEORGES: She would have been better off if the Germans had executed her.

SIMONE (*pleading for help*): That's the place where their heads get so big and the spit runs out of their mouth, Monsieur Chavez. They tie people up there!

MAYOR (*forcefully*): Madame, I shall make it undeniably clear at the proceedings in Tours just what this child's real motives were. Be quiet, Simone, we all know you acted out of patriotic motives.

123

MADAME SOUPEAU (*bursts out*): Ah! The little *Petroleuse* a national saint: is that the plan? France is saved: France burns. Here the German tanks, here Simone Machard, daughter of the day-laborer.

CAPTAIN FETAIN: Your past, Monsieur, is not of the kind which will dispose the judges of the new France to give your testimony much weight. Nor has the way to Tours become particularly safe for a person of your sort.

MAURICE (*eagerly*): Now I see what you're up to! You're trying to whitewash Saint-Martin of the accusation that there were any Frenchmen here.

MADAME SOUPEAU: Frenchmen? (*Taking hold of* SIMONE *and shaking her.*) Are you trying to teach us what it means to be patriotic? The Soupeaus have owned this Hostelry for two hundred years. (*To all present:*) Do you want to see a patriot? (*Pointing to* CAPTAIN FETAIN.) Here he is. We are quite capable of telling you when war is needed and when peace is best. Do you want to do something for France? All right. *We* are France. Is that understood?

CAPTAIN FETAIN: You're exerting yourself, Marie. . . .(*To the* MAYOR:) Why don't you put an end to it and have the Machard girl led away, Monsieur!

MAYOR: *I? You* seem to have assumed the power *here,* Monsieur. (*He turns to go.*)

SIMONE (*frightened*): Don't go away, Monsieur!

MAYOR (*helpless*): Chin up, Simone! (*He stumbles off, broken.*)

MADAME SOUPEAU (*during a silence, to* CAPTAIN FETAIN): Get this scandal over with, Honoré!

CAPTAIN FETAIN (*to the* POLICEMAN): I take responsibility here.

The POLICEMAN *takes hold of* SIMONE.

SIMONE (*softly, in uttermost fear*): Not to the Gray House!

ROBERT: You filthy pigs! (*He starts for the* POLICEMAN.)

MAURICE (*restraining him*): Don't be a fool, Robert. There's nothing more we can do for her. They've got the police on their side, and the Germans. Poor Simone, too many enemies for her.

MADAME SOUPEAU: Simone, get your things.

SIMONE *looks around. Her friends are silent, their eyes turned toward the ground. She goes into the supply shed, bewildered.*

MADAME SOUPEAU (*half to the employees, quietly, in an explanatory way*): This child is not only insubordinate, but utterly unable to accept authority. It is our distressing duty to see that she learns discipline.

SIMONE *returns with a very tiny suitcase, her apron under her arm. She hands the apron to* MADAME SOUPEAU.

MADAME SOUPEAU: And now you will open your suitcase so that we can all see what you are taking with you.

SOUPEAU: Is that necessary, Maman?

One of the Gray Ladies has already opened the tiny suitcase. She removes Simone's book.

SIMONE: Not my book!

The Gray Lady hands the book to MADAME SOUPEAU.

MADAME SOUPEAU: It belongs to the Hostelry.

SOUPEAU: I gave it to her.

MADAME SOUPEAU: It didn't do her much good. (*To* SIMONE:) Take your leave of the personnel now, Simone.

SIMONE: Good-bye, Monsieur Georges.

GEORGES: Will you be brave, Simone?

SIMONE: Of course, Monsieur Georges.

MAURICE: Be sure you stay well now.

SIMONE: Yes, Maurice.

GEORGES: Simone . . . I won't forget your cousin: the one with the dreams.

SIMONE smiles at him. She looks toward the roof of the garage. The light grows dimmer. Music fades in to announce the appearance of the ANGEL. SIMONE *looks at the roof of the garage, she sees the* ANGEL *there.*

ANGEL:
> Daughter of France, be not afraid.
> No man who fights her shall outlast God's Maid.
> The hand raised against thee in violence
>
> Will wither in consequence.
> Whither thou goest, it matters nought
> For where thou art, there France is brought.
> And after a little time we shall see
> France rise again in majesty.

The ANGEL *disappears, the full light returns. The Gray Ladies grasp* SIMONE *by the arm.* SIMONE *kisses* MAURICE *and* ROBERT, *and is led off. The others look on in silence.*

SIMONE (*turning in despair at the courtyard gate*): No, no! I won't go! Why don't you help me! Not to that place! André! André! André! (*She is dragged away.*)

MADAME SOUPEAU: My drops, Henri.

SOUPEAU (*darkly*): Maurice, Robert, Georges, Père Gustave, get to your work! And don't forget that we are at peace now.

SOUPEAU and CAPTAIN FETAIN lead MADAME SOUPEAU into the Hostelry. MAURICE and ROBERT leave through the courtyard gate. PERE GUSTAVE rolls out a tire to

127

Bertolt Brecht

be mended. GEORGES *inspects his lame arm. The sky begins to grow red.* PERE GUSTAVE *points it out to* GEORGES. SOUPEAU *storms out of the Hostelry.*

SOUPEAU: Maurice, Robert! Find out what's burning. At once! (*He goes off.*)

PERE GUSTAVE: It must be the assembly hall. The refugees! It seems they've learned something after all.

GEORGES: They can't have arrived at the Gray House yet. Simone will see the fire from the car.